My Adventures
in Widowhood

SIMON AND SCHUSTER

Harry

Virginia Graham

New York · London · Toronto · Sydney · Tokyo

Published by Simon and Schuster
A Division of Simon & Schuster Inc.
Simon & Schuster Building
Rockefeller Center
1230 Avenue of the Americas
New York, NY 10020
SIMON AND SCHUSTER and colophon are registered trademarks
of Simon & Schuster Inc.

Designed by Helen L. Granger/Levavi & Levavi
Manufactured in the United States of America

5   7   9   10   8   6   4
Library of Congress Cataloging-in-Publication Data
Graham, Virginia, date.
Life after Harry: my adventures in widowhood / Virginia Graham.
p.   cm.
Bibliography: p.
ISBN 0-671-63816-5
1. Graham, Virginia, date–   2. Widows—United States—
Biography.   I. Title.
HQ1058.5.U5G72   1988
306.8′8—dc19
87-28766
CIP

The author wishes to thank the following authors and publishers for permission to quote from the books and articles listed:

Abigail Van Buren, "Dear Abby," © 1986, Universal Press Syndicate, all rights reserved.

Peter McWilliams, *How to Survive the Loss of a Love*, New York, Bantam Books (by arrangement with Leo Press), 1977.

To Lynn, Jan and Stephen,
with whom I expect
to spend my future

Contents

Acknowledgments

Writing this book has been one of the most important tasks of my life, and I didn't do it alone.

I want to thank my marvelous literary agent, Jane Dystel, who represented me with skill and dedication. And my editor at Simon & Schuster, Laurie Lister, whose faith in me made this book a reality. And I want to thank Catherine Whitney, who has been my writing collaborator throughout the creation of this book. Catherine sat with me for many long hours, taping and editing my words, putting up with me, and laughing along with me at the funny twists and turns of life.

Of course, thanks are also due to all of my friends and acquaintances whose words and experiences fill the pages of this book. It is through them that I have discovered most of what I know. The greatest resource of my life has been the presence of people who have shared their stories and experiences with me.

However, many of my friends have been *overly* generous with their advice as I wrote this book. I would like to mention a few of them here; these are the people without whom I never would have considered doing myself in.

To my friend who said kindly, "If this book is about Harry, I'll vomit. I've had enough already."

To another friend, who suggested, "I think this book should be about *pain*. Make them cry a lot and feel their sadness." (Yes, and my editor would have been crying a lot if I had listened to that advice.)

To the person who said, "Are you really going to tell the truth? You wouldn't do that, would you, and ruin your career?"

To the person or persons who will most certainly say when they read this book, "You meant me, didn't you? How could you have betrayed my confidence like that?" (No, it's not you . . . your story is so unbelievable that if I had written about you, this book would have been published as fiction.)

To my grandchildren, who tried very hard to hide their astonishment when they exclaimed, "They're *paying* you to write this book?"

To my skeptical friend who said, "How do you think poor dear departed Harry would feel if he knew the things you were writing about him?" (I think Harry is laughing his head off, wherever he is.)

To my butcher, my grocer and my dry cleaner, who each said, "Of course, you're going to mention me."

To my doctor, who said with a worried frown, "I hope they don't wait too long to publish this book."

To all the blind dates who have made living alone a veritable paradise.

And, from the bottom of my heart, I want to thank all the women of achievement who have made it on their own, against all odds—women who are living their lives with spirit and dignity. They've shown me that anything is possible . . . that if life sends me a package C.O.D., I'll always have the resources to pay for it.

◈ *1* ◈

Is There Life After Harry?

Let me introduce myself. My name is Virginia Graham, and like you, I am a woman alone.

Eight years ago Harry Guttenberg, my husband of forty-four years, died and I became a widow. The experience took me completely by surprise. Harry had been ill for several years, so the actual prospect of his death was not unexpected. What *was* unexpected was the way I found myself reacting.

For the first time in my life I felt real fear. I would wake up in the night trembling in the dark, my head spinning with unnamed terrors. For the first time in my life I felt depressed. Some days it was hard to drag my body out of bed. I would sit for hours, unable to work or think or laugh. For the first time in my life I began to feel old, over the hill. I thought, "No man will ever look at me again . . . no one will want to hire me . . . it's all over for me."

These strange emotions running rampant inside me were completely out of character. Before widowhood I had been happy, secure and full of life. Suddenly I was a basket case. What was happening to me?

I called a therapist friend and confessed, "I feel awful and I don't know how to stop it."

"What you're experiencing is completely normal," she explained to me. "It's grief."

"I can't bear it. There must be something I can do."

She suggested several things: "You can give your wounds the time they need to heal. You can stop feeling guilty that Harry's dead and you're alive. And you can build your resources. Learn to accept yourself the way you are. Accept your future as an opportunity."

"Are you sure I can do all that?" I asked. It seemed like a tall order.

"You must if you really want to live," she said.

I realized with a start that I *did* want to live. More than anything, I wanted to live. And I began my recovery. It wasn't easy, though. I sought in vain for books that would give me comfort and inspiration and there were few to be found. My friends wanted to help, but they were ill-equipped to do so. There isn't much information available about how to help a friend cope with grief. Eventually I made it, though, and today, at the age of seventy-four, eight years after Harry's death, I can honestly say I am making it on my own. And I am really very happy.

This book is my gift to you. I want to share my life, the good times, the bad times and the hilarious experiences I've had. If I can make even a small dent in the grief and confusion I know you're feeling, it will make me very happy.

Just a Little Girl Talk

I feel very comfortable writing this book because I have spent the last thirty-five years talking to women. I started in television in 1951, with a little show called *Food for Thought*. In 1961 I created *Girl Talk*, a women's program that was the first of its kind, followed by the *Virginia Graham Show*, which was on the air from 1970 to 1973. These were all "talk shows" for women and I loved doing them. They were gratifying, funny and very often outrageous.

During the past few years I have given literally hundreds of talks to women's groups across the country. I have shared their laughter and their tears. I have always been grateful for my work, which takes me out on the road. I feel I have developed a common bond with women in every part of this country, and I feel welcomed into the towns and homes of people whose lives I have come to share.

Women view me as a friend—and that's just what I want to be. I once got the sweetest note from a woman in a small rural town, who wrote, "I wish you were my neighbor." I considered that the highest compliment anyone could pay me. I never wanted to be just another celebrity, sitting on a pedestal. My ambition always was to be a friend, a listening ear to the women of America.

On occasion, through the years, I've shaken my head and thought, "Isn't it the most amazing thing that a little Great Neck housewife could have ended up this way?"

But life works in mysterious ways and I have been especially blessed.

After I became a widow I became more aware of how many women there are in America who have lost their husbands and are trying to make it alone. I have listened to them and learned that their experiences are no different from mine. In fact, I first began to think about writing this book after I had an encounter with one such woman.

She was recently widowed and having a hard time holding back the tears as she spoke. "Virginia," she asked, "how did you ever find a way to get along without Harry after he died? I can't seem to shake these awful feelings. I feel like I'm walking around with half of myself missing. I wish you could sit with me and tell me how I'm ever going to make it."

Her words kept echoing in my ears, long after we spoke. I could certainly feel her pain, remembering how lost I felt after Harry died. And I thought about all the conversations I've had with widows across the country, many of them literally fighting for their lives against their depressed, sometimes suicidal feelings. I knew I could help these women and others find their way.

The Ten Amendments for Widows

Most of us have lived all our lives based on the image of being one half of a couple. We saw ourselves following a certain pattern—we'd get married, have children and live together, happily ever after, with our husbands.

But now unexpectedly we find ourselves asking, "What do I do now?" There are no guidelines for women like us to follow and the old rules just don't seem to apply anymore. It's scary!

What we widows need is a new set of directions, amendments, if you will, to the constitution we lived in accordance with before our husbands died. So I wrote "The Ten Amendments for Widows." They will form the basis of what I have to say in this book, the guidelines for women who want to live full and happy lives alone.

The Ten Amendments are

1. Yes, there *is* life after what's-his-name. You don't have to jump into the grave after your husband. You can be a full person on your own.
2. Never settle for a man simply because he's still breathing. You can demand the best in all of your relationships.
3. Don't let the world take advantage of you because you're alone. Beware of scams. If it sounds too good to be true, it's too good to be true.
4. Your children are separate people. Don't make them your life and don't let them make you theirs.
5. You can be beautiful . . . the face you wake up with in the morning is not necessarily the one you're stuck with for the rest of the day.
6. You can find out again just how much fun life can be as a "merry widow" in the world.
7. When one door closes, another one opens . . . and new opportunities are knocking all the time.
8. You can love living alone . . . and discover the delicious pleasures of a single life.
9. Your senior years can be golden, not brass. You're getting older, but you're also getting better.

10. You never have to feel ashamed to be alone in the world. A table for one can be a grand adventure.

These are your ten new rules for living. I learned to believe in them and you can too.

Perhaps the first one is the hardest of all . . . the understanding that there *is* life after Harry . . . and Tom . . . and Dick . . . and Bill. When you can really believe that, you're on your way.

'Til Death Do Us Part

When I said my wedding vows I never imagined that death really would "do us part." It's not something a happy young bride thinks about. I adored Harry. He was the most interesting man I had ever met and I was initially so taken with him that I agreed to marry him only two weeks after we had met.

I was also dazzled by the idea of marrying an "older man"—I was twenty-two and Harry was thirty. (Of course, I had no idea how *much* older Harry was. He lied to me about his age for forty-four years, and it was only when I saw his death certificate that I learned he was really thirty-seven when we married. I really had to laugh when I made that discovery!)

I can't imagine what life would have been like without Harry—we were literally joined at the hip. We went everywhere together, shared every thought and experience. Even after I eventually launched a successful career, our relationship never changed. I could never get over the way Harry encouraged my career. He was so proud of me and always accepted with great grace the admiration I received from people. He never minded hearing people say, "You're so lucky to have a wife like Virginia," because he agreed with them. To Harry I was always the most beautiful woman in the room—and the most fun. He was never bored with me.

And I needed him. It's a good thing that Harry became so involved in my career because I never could have done it without him. For one thing, he kept my books, since I had no head at all for managing money. Harry was an expert at charming the bank officers. They would call and say, "Mr. Guttenberg, we don't quite understand. Your wife made a large deposit just two days ago and now she's overdrawn. We'll have to take some action here." After Harry had picked himself up off the floor, he would say smoothly, "I don't understand it either, but why don't you come over for a drink. I'm sure we can straighten this out." I'm certain Harry kept me out of jail and saved my life many times with his charm.

Also, Harry answered every letter I ever got. He had beautiful handwriting; mine looked like bird scratchings. And he had a talent for writing the most wonderful letters. In fact, this talent led to a very funny incident with one of my fans. Verna Corsey lived in Philadelphia. She wrote me many long, beautiful letters—they were veritable tomes. Over the years, we developed a close and dear pen pal relationship, except it was Harry who wrote all the letters, signing my name with great flourish at the end.

One year Clairol, for whom I was working at the time, sent me to a convention in Philadelphia. And Harry said, "Wouldn't it be nice, after all these years, if we could call Verna and take her out to dinner while we're there. She's been such an ardent fan." I said, "Harry, that's a great idea." And I called Verna.

"Oh," she moaned, "I can't meet you. My teeth aren't ready."

"What do you mean?"

"I'm having new teeth made," she admitted. "I can't have you see me like this."

I said, "Verna, don't be silly. Wear your old teeth. What difference does it make?"

"I'm so nervous."

"Verna," I said sternly, "please stop this nonsense. We've got to meet, and that's that."

So we met at the hotel, and when Verna walked up to me, I thought she looked exactly the way Verna Corsey should look—sweet and plump, with a sparkle of excitement in her eyes.

"Oh, Virginia," she cried, "I can't believe I'm really meeting you!" Then she turned and gave Harry the most dazzling smile of adoration I had ever seen. "And this is Harry," she said in a tone that approached reverence. "I've always longed to meet you because I've never heard a woman rave so much about her husband the way Virginia has raved about you in her letters. You sound like the best husband a woman ever had."

I thought I would die! All those years Harry had been answering my mail and writing glowingly about himself. I shot him a killer look and said sweetly, "Yes, Verna, it's all true. I just don't know what I'd do without Harry."

After dinner we invited Verna up to our suite for coffee, and while we were sitting and talking, I braced myself for the inevitable. What was the one thing Verna Corsey was going to want from me? My autograph, of course, and I knew this was going to be a disaster because my autograph was really Harry's autograph.

Sure enough, Verna pulled five pictures out of her bag. "I hope it won't be an imposition, but I promised my friends and my mother that I would get these pictures autographed for them."

"Of course," I said, smiling. I grabbed the pictures and jumped to my feet. "Oh, darn. Harry, would you come into the bedroom with me for a moment? My zipper is loose and I need your help."

Verna jumped up too. "I'll help you."

"No, no, Harry can do it. We won't be a minute."

So we went into the bedroom and Harry sat down and autographed the pictures for Verna.

Many years later, when Harry was hospitalized, I called Verna and said, "It's very lonesome not having Harry around the house."

She sympathized. "I know. And what a help he was to you, too—answering all your mail."

I choked. "What do you mean?"

"Virginia," she said, laughing, "you don't think for one minute that I thought it was you who wrote those letters? I knew all along it was Harry!"

So much for subterfuge.

Harry was an excessive man—he loved to drink, had a hearty appetite, and he smoked five packs of cigarettes a day. I used to tell a joke that one time I passed Harry on the street but I didn't recognize him because he wasn't smoking a cigarette. A doctor once told me, "If Harry can live this long doing what I've told everyone not to do, I'm in the wrong business."

But I guess it finally caught up with him. Harry was ill for several years before he died, but he was a wonderful patient and I never once heard him complain. Looking back, I'd have to say that Harry was heroic about his illness.

During the last two years of his life, he lived at the Actors' Home in Englewood, New Jersey. I had to continue working to support us, so I could no longer care for his daily needs. But I visited him twice a week and spoke to him on the phone twice a day. It was a terrible adjustment. As anyone who has put a loved one in a nursing home knows, no matter how wonderful the place, no matter how right the decision, there is a lot of guilt.

Near the end of his life Harry was on dialysis, but he was stable. At that time I was in a play in Maryland called *My Daughter, Your Son,* and I spoke with him by phone every day. But one day I received the call from Harry's doctor that I'd been dreading. Harry was failing fast. "My God," I cried, "I'm coming right in."

They asked me, "Should we use extraordinary measures to keep him alive?"

I don't believe in taking extraordinary measures. I think it is the highest form of cruelty to keep a body functioning when there's nothing left of the person inside. But I said, "Yes, until I get there. Please don't let Harry die until I get there."

I couldn't get a plane from Washington, so I took the train from Baltimore, and believe me, it was the longest train ride of my life. Before I left the station I called my best friend, Nan Goddard, and said, "Nan, please meet me at the hospital. Harry's failing."

I think God sends us special people to make our life on earth easier, and Nan was that for me. Her friendship saw me through a lot of hard times. While I was in Maryland, Nan had been visiting Harry every day.

The train finally arrived at Penn Station and I flew to the street, grabbed a taxi and got to the hospital just as Nan was arriving. We raced to the nurses' station on Harry's floor.

"Where is he?" I cried.

Nan grabbed my arm and pulled me down the corridor. "I know where he is, right in this room."

Before the nurse could stop me, I went in. Every bed was filled . . . with a stranger.

I turned around and opened my mouth, but no words came out. The nurse put her hand on my arm and said softly, "Miss Graham, I'm so sorry."

At that moment I was as overcome with sorrow as I have ever been in my entire life. I was too late to say good-bye to Harry. I was reminded of something Harry's nephew, who had never been married, once told me. He said, "The only thing that bothers me about not having married is that I will be alone when I die."

All this was running through my mind as I stood there. I felt I had betrayed Harry by leaving him to die alone. "Oh, Harry," I begged silently, "will you ever forgive me for this?"

Looking back, I realize that there was nothing I could have done, and the nurses assured me that Harry had not been conscious in the end anyway. In fact, I guess we all die alone whether there are loved ones with us or not. But it was a terrible moment.

This was a particularly difficult time for my family. My daughter, Lynn, had just lost her beloved husband shortly before Harry died. So mother and daughter were widowed together. We cried for ourselves and for each other. I must say that Lynn's courage and bravery were an inspiration, helping me immeasurably in bearing my own loss.

So, I said good-bye to Harry after forty-four years. His funeral was a small, quiet affair, and he was buried where he wanted to be, next to his mother and sisters. Today, when I go to visit his grave, I am always cheered by the fact that he's there with the people he loved so much.

Now, I chose a small funeral, but I think a funeral can be different things to different people—it's a very personal event. Some people throw a big party; others ask the deceased's friends and relatives to share stories. I once heard of a rabbi who said, in the middle of the funeral, "I didn't know this man as well as those of you who loved him all his life, so I would like a few of you to think about the deceased now and say a few words." He turned to the widow and said, "We'll start with you. If you had to describe your husband in one word, what would that word be?"

She sat for a moment thinking, and then she said with great solemnity, "Thrift."

The rabbi cleared his throat and asked the man next to her to continue. He also sat deep in thought for a moment before he answered, "His brother was worse."

I guess you have to be careful when you open up the funeral service to remarks from the loved ones!

Time to Move On

For the first few months after Harry died, I was obsessed with the past. I'd lie awake at night, replaying the scenes from our marriage . . . the birth of our daughter, Lynn . . . the way we laughed and played . . . Harry's funny little neuroses . . . the many trips we took together. I couldn't imagine how I'd be a person without him. After forty-four years it wasn't something I knew how to do.

My recovery was much like learning to walk all over again. It was learning to say "I" instead of "we." And as I told you earlier, that wasn't easy.

I realize now that recovery from grief means a lot more than just learning to get by. It means learning to be happy. Today I am a happy woman . . . a downright merry widow. I hope this book helps in a small way to open up that chance for you too.

❖ 2 ❖

Follow Your Heart

There I stood, staring at the grayest man I'd ever seen in my life. His hair was gray. His face was gray and etched with a pasty shadow that called to mind the expression "death warmed over." His clothes hung on him —gray, of course, and completely nondescript. Only his blue tie saved him from disappearing into the background of my friend's gray walls.

I felt my heart perform a small elevator crash of dismay. This was my blind date for the evening, and I knew at once that the blindness of this date belonged, most of all, to my friend, who had obviously set up this match with her eyes closed.

She had called me a few days earlier with great excitement. "Ginny, darling, you *must* come for dinner. I have this marvelous man for you. A widower. You have to meet him."

"What's he like?"

"Oh, he's a fine, fine man. A lovely person and very successful."

And so I arrived, full of vim, vigor and high expectations and ran smack into Mr. Gray. To call the evening excrutiatingly painful would be an understatement of the highest order. You see, his personality matched his outward coloring. He never opened his mouth the entire evening. I tried desperately to make conversation with him, but he just sat with a glassy, fixed stare. At one point during dinner, when he asked me to pass the salt, I felt like giving him a standing ovation for finally breaking out of his shell.

The next day I called my friend and said, "I really appreciate what you did. I know your heart was in the right place, but your eyes must have been closed at the time you made this deal."

And do you know what she said to me? She said, "You should be so lucky as to have a man like that."

I was stunned and later, when I thought about it more, I was angry. What kind of remark was that for a woman to make to another woman? A widow may feel deflated, but she has at least a little ego left. Maybe she's just beginning to find herself, just beginning to think she's really not so bad, and then she's told that she *should be so lucky* as to be introduced to a boring, dull man like that!

I felt that my friend was really saying, "Who the hell are you, Virginia Graham, to think that you can get an exciting, wonderful man at your stage in life?"

And, after hearing this story, you may be thinking, "Aha! My worst suspicions are confirmed. I cannot bear the idea of dating again, of subjecting myself to that kind of humiliation." But before you decide to skip this chapter completely, I'd like to say one thing to you.

If you are a woman, a widow, who deep down inside would really like to meet another man, don't ever feel ashamed of that need. I know it's easy to let your fears take over, to listen to the nagging voice in your head that says, "I'm too old. Who's going to look at me? Who's going to want me?" But turn it off. Tune in to a different channel that tells you, "I don't have to settle for anything less than what I really want. I deserve happiness."

Just because a *body* asks you out, don't think you have to be grateful. If you love yourself at all, you'll see that you're worthy of a good man.

I have a friend who goes out with a man who is totally wrong for her. Whenever I see them together I am absolutely amazed that she would even be seen with him in public. This man has no class at all, and a spender he's not. He thinks the subway is a private limousine that's kind enough to take on other people. After this relationship had been going on for some time, I finally got up the nerve to ask my friend about it.

"I don't know how to put this delicately," I said. "But what on earth do you see in this man?"

"He's not so bad."

"Not so bad? Are you kidding? Darling, this man makes Attila the Hun look like a charmer."

She shrugged. "At least I'm not alone. People will see us out together."

"You *want* people to see you together?"

"It's better than being alone."

What is it, I wonder, that makes us so desperate that we're willing to settle for even the most miserable relationship?

I never realized until Harry died how big the world is

and how empty a room can be. My world had been very small and there was always another person in the room. I had often wondered about women who were widowed and took it so terribly when I knew they hadn't had great marriages. Some women will put up with almost anything rather than be alone.

Don't get me wrong. I think it's perfectly all right to want to find another man. But you have to approach the task with pride in yourself. And you must have a sense of humor about dating again. I know that in the years since Harry died I've had my share of bizarre dating experiences. If I took them seriously, I'd be a basket case by now.

Often, I have to remind myself that my friends who orchestrate these events mean well and have my best interests at heart. That's not always easy to see.

My date with "toothless Henry" was typical. A friend had arranged a foursome with a man she told me was a perfect match for me.

"You know how much I love you," she said. "And I think I've found the man for you."

So I said, "Okay, ready or not, here I come."

"Listen, Virginia," she then said. "Do you mind if I'm very frank with you?"

"No, not at all."

"You have beautiful jewelry and you look well in it."

"So?" I couldn't imagine what she was getting at.

"It could scare some men away."

I laughed at that. "I don't know that I want the type of man who would be scared away by jewelry."

She frowned. "Virginia, don't kid about this. Take my advice. Wear that pretty black suit with the little lace collar. I love that on you. And wear little pearl earrings—"

"Wait a minute," I cried. "You want me to wear *little* pearl earrings? I'd look like I had an acne infection. I don't own little earrings. I have *very* big earlobes!"

"Okay," she conceded, "but wear pearls and maybe a pearl ring. That's it."

I wasn't happy with this arrangement. "No one will recognize me dressed like that," I complained. "We won't get a good table at the restaurant."

"Just listen to me. I know what I'm talking about."

So I asked, "What's he like, this man of my dreams?"

"Well," she said, "you know my taste."

"Yes." I wrinkled my nose. "But I'm going anyway."

So I went to the restaurant where I was to meet them, and in walked my friend wearing the most exquisite cocktail dress I had ever seen. And her shoulders were raw from the weight of the emerald earrings hanging from her earlobes. And she was unable to bend her finger for the size of the ring she was wearing. Meanwhile, there I was in this little black number that made me look like the maid.

"Aren't you afraid you'll scare people away with all that jewelry?" I mumbled to her as we walked into the restaurant. She shot me a look.

In the foyer I spotted my date, Henry, and the first thing that flashed into my mind was that he looked like a poster boy for Forest Lawn.

I'm a big woman and I need a big man, not someone who will be swept away by the first strong gust of wind. Henry looked parched, like he had just barely survived a long desert trek. And when he opened his mouth I saw acres of black gums. He had but four teeth in the front. And he was a doctor!

Throughout the meal Henry couldn't take his eyes off my friend. He didn't seem to be the least bit intimidated by her jewelry. And all this time people were coming over to our table to ask for my autograph.

Finally, Henry turned to me and said, "Why are all these people asking for your autograph?".

"Well," I said modestly, "I'm on television."

This sparked something in him. "You are? What do you do on television?"

"For many years I had my own show," I began, "and now I—"

He cut me off. "I *hate* television. The only thing I've ever liked is *Kojak*."

By now I was beginning to get fed up, so I gave him my most charming smile and said sweetly, "Oh, dear, had I known, I would have shaved my head, but I wasn't told."

Meanwhile, my friend was kicking me under the table (I've still got the marks from her heels) and staring daggers at me. But I couldn't help myself. It was just an evening of torture.

Finally it was time to leave and I couldn't wait to get home. I grabbed my friend's arm. "I'll go with you."

"Oh, no," she said. "The doctor wants to take you home." The doctor would have liked to get an emergency call on his beeper!

But we left together and got into the taxi. I never knew how cold steel was until I found my body pressed against the door of that cab. Henry was pressed against the door on the other side. God forbid that we should touch!

As the cab approached my building, before it had even stopped, I had the door open and was flying out, calling behind me, "Good night . . . thank you." I raced through the corridor. I couldn't wait to get upstairs.

Do you know that some people will frown at me for complaining about my date with toothless Henry? They'll say, "What's the matter with you? He's living. He's a man. Don't turn down anybody." Well, that's just ridiculous. I deserve to enjoy my relationships—and so do you. Don't settle for a man just because he's still breathing!

It's natural to wonder whether or not you still possess some of the same charm and desirability that you once had. It's natural to be nervous as you embark upon a new social life. But don't settle for the crumbs.

Take the First Step

Perhaps the hardest thing of all is taking the first step in deciding to get out and meet men. You're out of practice and it may seem that the most terrifying thing in the world is walking into a room alone and meeting new people. There are times when you're going to feel like everyone else in the world is younger, better looking and more desirable than you are.

I have to understand and cry with and console any woman who says, "I just can't go out and look. He's got to find me. I never called a man for a date. I always went out with a man when he asked me. I've never invited a man over for dinner. I just can't do it. I lived with one man all my life and I'm not used to these things."

But I also have to say, *That's over!* It's not going to be like that anymore. He's gone and you're not going with him. You're going to have to learn to live again in the best way you can.

I've found that asking a man for dinner doesn't have to be such a terrible trauma, especially when you use your friends for support.

I met a wonderful man at a dinner party once and we

hit it off beautifully. I wasn't in the habit of calling men for dates, but I was very interested in seeing him again. So I called a friend and said, "I want you to come to dinner next week. I'm going to invite this man and please tell your husband to keep his mouth shut—no jokes or remarks."

Once that was settled, I called the man. "Listen," I said casually, "I enjoyed meeting you so much the other night and I'm having friends over for dinner. I'd like it very much if you could come."

Now, it didn't kill me to extend this invitation—and he was happy to accept.

Yes, I assure you, *you* can meet another man if that's what you want. It doesn't make a difference if you're shy. If you have arthritis. If the weight has established a permanent residence on your hips. If you're past the blush of youth. Anything is possible if you have a deeply happy sense of your own worth and specialness in the world. There's no beauty that is as great as the glow that comes from a woman who truly loves herself and other people. Her light shines through.

I once knew a woman who was, by most standards, unattractive. But at parties and other gatherings she was always surrounded by men. What was the quality that drew them to her? She definitely had an *aura* about her, a way of being that made men feel special. It wasn't so much the way she looked as the way she *was*. She was a great inspiration to me because I really saw that the force of her beauty was reflected through her enthusiasm for life, her interest in others and the quiet certainty that she held about her own self.

If you want to attract another man, use this woman as a model. And remember these points:

1. BE NATURAL. Most men find openness and honesty refreshing. They're not interested in coy games and women who put on airs. Be yourself (remember that self you love!), and if a man doesn't enjoy you just the way you are, you don't want him anyway.

2. LISTEN WITH YOUR EYES. Listening is not something that happens with the ears. It's the whole communication—and your eyes are the windows that reflect your interest. Good communication happens when you look a man straight in the eyes while you're talking with him. It tells him that you're completely intent on him... you're not thinking about what else is going on in the room. Maybe this takes a little practice—after many years of marriage, you and your husband probably developed a kind of shorthand, and you may not be used to looking at men so boldly. But it's a great compliment when you look him in the eye and listen with your whole body.

3. BE INTERESTED... DON'T PRY. Know the difference between interest and prying. For heaven's sake, stay out of areas where you don't belong. If you begin prying, you're sending up warning flares that a man can spot a mile away. He'll begin to feel trapped and hemmed in by your interest. I don't know what it is about women, but we have the uncanny ability to scare a man away before he's even said two words to us. Don't be planning your wedding when the hellos are barely out of your mouth.

4. DON'T BE A NAG. Nagging is an ugly thing. It suffocates men and I think it's a valid reason for a man to run like hell if a woman is a nag. I've known too

many women who have lost their men by nagging them right out of the house. When you nag a man it's the same as telling him, "I don't like you the way you are . . . I want you to change."

5. BE INDEPENDENT. It's mathematically impossible for two to become one, so keep your independence and allow him his. The greatest and most successful relationships occur when each partner has freedom. The desire to cling to a man is merely a statement of your own insecurity, the very thing that you're trying so hard to overcome.

First-Date Etiquette

I'm not Emily Post. I'm not even Miss Manners. If you know me at all, you know that I tend to skirt some of the norms of etiquette—my mouth was never sent to finishing school. But for me, etiquette is simply the way you behave that makes the person you're with feel relaxed and welcome. And that's something I take seriously.

It's possible that the last time you went on a date was forty years ago, when you met your husband. And there are some things about first dates that never change: the sweaty palms, the nervous stomach and the absolute certainty that he won't like you. Go ahead and feel all these things. But don't forget to add a healthy dose of self-esteem to the stew.

It's just a date. Say that to yourself over and over again. It's just a date. Don't make more of it than it is—a pleasant evening out with a man.

Here's my list of dos and don'ts for going out with a man for the first time:

1. Be punctual. It's really a terrible insult to be late getting ready for a date. It conveys a lack of respect for your companion. I know women who always have to use the bathroom immediately after a date arrives. Why can't they take care of that before he comes?

   A friend of mine disputed this. "I like to be a little late," she told me. "I wouldn't want him to think I'm too eager."

   "Too eager? What are you talking about? You already have the date. Aren't you eager to be with him?"

   "Well, yes."

   "Then let him know it. It'll make him feel good."

2. Don't fish for compliments. If he tells you that you look wonderful, that's fine. Say thank you. But never ask, "Do you like this dress?" "What do you think of my new hairstyle?" Men hate to be put on the spot that way . . . and what do you expect him to say, that you look awful? Keep your insecurities to yourself!

3. Don't talk about your husband. Your date knows you're a widow, and he's probably already a bit nervous about the comparison you might be making between him and your husband. I know women who might as well ask for a table for three in restaurants because they take their dead husbands out with them on every date. It's not just the obvious things I'm talking about, either. It's the subtle little things. For example, your date orders a steak and you casually comment, "Oh, Bob never touched red meat." Keep a lid on it.

4. Don't be critical. Let him feel that he's pleasing you

and that there's nothing you'd rather be doing than spending this evening with him. Don't criticize his clothes, his choice of restaurants or his personal habits.

Of course, by the same token, you are *never* obliged to spend one minute more with a man than you can tolerate. If you find yourself with a blind date who is insulting or offensive, you may find a way to politely excuse yourself from the evening.

5. Keep your distance. Men can smell a desperate woman a hundred miles away. Remember that you're on a date; it's not a prelude to marriage. If you like this man and he doesn't suggest a second date, you're going to be absolutely *dying* to say, "Will I see you again?" But try to control the urge. Rather, say graciously, "I really enjoyed myself so much . . . and I look forward to seeing you again."

Who Is Mr. Right?

But who is the "right man" and how do you know he's out there for you? To begin with, some widows are just afraid to look. They canonize their late husbands and then use that as an excuse for not facing the future. I've known women like that, who are really very lonely, and frankly I find it very sad to watch them carrying their departed husband's alleged perfection around with them like a badge. They decide not to meet other men because, after all, how could anyone ever measure up to their husbands?

An acquaintance of mine was married for many years to a man who had, to put it very kindly, flaws. In fact, during the course of their marriage, she was often ready to throw in the towel and leave him, but she never did. Then he died and suddenly he became a saint. I listened to her descriptions of this newly canonized man and I was flabbergasted. Finally, when I could stand no more, I blurted out one day, "Have you been married more than once?"

She was puzzled. "Virginia, you've known me all my life. What kind of question is that?"

As delicately as I could (and I admit that delicacy is not my strong suit), I said, "This man that you're describing is certainly not the man I knew. What is this, *Fantasy Island?* I think it's lovely that you were married to such a wonderful person, but I'm telling you that it's no one I ever met."

She was pretty angry with me for saying that, but I held fast to my belief that it's nonsense to live in a pretend world.

I know another woman who was married to a P-I-G . . . that's right, he was a pig. If there was anything good about this man, I certainly never saw it. Long after he had died I asked my friend one day, "Have you ever thought about getting married again?"

"How could I!" she cried. "Not after the way Ralph loved me. He treated me like a princess, Virginia. He waited on me hand and foot. I could never find anyone like Ralph."

When she said this, I thought to myself, "I'm in the presence of either a psychotic or a very creative scenario writer." But she was so convinced, I realized it would be pointless for me to disabuse her of the notion. "You're right," I told her. "You'll never find another man like Ralph." At least that was the truth. There couldn't have been another man on earth as bad as he was.

So stop glorifying your husband and be honest with

yourself. Do you want another man? If the answer is yes —and there are very few women who would say no to the possibility of romance in their lives—then figure out what you want and take steps to find him.

Unfortunately you won't be able to accomplish this by sitting alone in your house waiting for him to come knocking on your door. You have to make the effort and that might mean doing things you never dreamed you'd do.

That's the way I felt when I found myself sitting in the very plush waiting room of a video dating service. I had worked up the courage to call for an appointment and here's how it came about. I was talking to a friend about suggestions I could make in this book for meeting men and she said, "How about dating services?"

Immediately my mind flashed on a picture of a dirty little walk-up with dusty old desks and a plump, grandmotherly matchmaker. "You mean marriage bureaus?"

She laughed. "Virginia, you have no idea the scope of services available for meeting men."

I was skeptical. "For younger women, maybe, but do you really think that an older woman can find a man through these services? I won't hang by my fingernails until they find *me* a man, that's for sure."

"Well," she said logically, "you'll never know until you go see for yourself. What do you have to lose?"

She was right about that, so I got up the nerve to call for an appointment with a video dating service. When I walked into the office I was impressed to find a beautiful waiting room and an office that extended the full length of the floor. And sitting there were five of the most gorgeous young women I have ever seen. They all came over to me and made me feel completely welcome. Right away some of my initial nervousness had passed. Then, out came the owner in a beautiful, chic outfit, and she was stunning.

I noticed that there were a couple of people seated in the foyer and there was one man there who, I must say, didn't look like he'd live long enough to go out on a date. But I was encouraged because there seemed to be people of all ages.

With this particular service, the customer does the choosing. I was shown into an enormous library with huge albums that members could look through at their leisure to find the person who appealed to them.

I was fascinated. "Is this dating or mating?" I asked. "How many people meet a mate here?"

The owner replied, "Not everyone who comes in is looking for marriage, but a high percentage of them do find a mate here."

"So," I asked, "what happens if you find someone in the albums that you would like to meet?"

"Then you look at the video. One of our people interviews each man and woman on tape."

The thought of being on video sent chills up my spine ... a rather strange reaction for a woman who has lived most of her life on film! But I went ahead and began to look through the albums until I found a man I liked. I read his application and learned that Shelley was sixty-two years old, smoked a pipe and didn't drink. On tape Shelley was a very charming man. "What if I wanted to meet him?" I asked.

"You'd fill out a card and then we'd let him know that someone is interested, and he'd come in and see your tape."

It all sounded very easy, but I had my doubts. "Listen," I said to her honestly, "your literature says you have people from twenty-four to eighty. That's ridiculous. Have you ever matched up two older people? Maybe an older man with a younger woman, but how about the older women? All you hear about these days is that men want to go out with only younger women."

She admitted that I had a point, but added, "You'd be surprised how many young men we see are looking for older women. An older woman is often not ashamed to show that she wants a man around. She knows what the score is and she makes a man feel comfortable."

I visited several dating services in the course of my research, but I never honestly expected anything to come of it for me. To my amazement, however, a woman from one of the services called me a couple of weeks later. "Virginia," she said, "I've got the perfect man for you. Of all the men who have ever come in, Frank has been our favorite."

"Why, that's wonderful," I replied.

"Now, I must tell you in all honesty," she went on, "that we've had a little problem with Frank. We've sent him out with four women and none of them have worked out. He's what you'd call a little picky."

I said bravely, "I guess that's where I come in."

She told me she would call Frank to see if he was interested and call me back.

"Virginia," she said when she called again, "I've got some good news and some bad news."

"What's the good news?"

"He thinks you're the most wonderful woman in the world. He says he's adored you from afar all his life. And he's just thrilled with the prospect of meeting you."

"My God," I cried. "He sounds perfect. What could be bad?"

"The bad news is that he just met another woman."

"Oh," I gulped, deflated. "That is bad news. But why don't I meet him anyway. He can give me his input on dating services for my book."

So, a few days later the phone rang and this gorgeous voice came on that absolutely made my heart stop. It was Frank.

"What a beautiful voice you have," I told him. "You should be in radio."

"That's good, since I *am* in radio," he laughed.

Then he told me how he had watched me on television over the years and how much he admired me, and there I sat like a schoolgirl, blushing over the phone.

"Tell me something," he said after a while. "Why would Virginia Graham be using a dating service? You must be fighting them off."

I laughed out loud. "Yes, I'm fighting *him* off in droves. But seriously, it's sometimes harder for me than it is for other women because so many men are intimidated by what they believe is my public success. It's the hardest thing in the world for successful women to meet men. It's funny, really. People think of me as this incredibly glamorous, worldly person when, really, I'm basically just a homebody."

You can see I was immediately taken with Frank; I opened up to him like a blooming flower. We talked on the phone for an hour, and during that time my heart was literally in my throat. Finally I said, "Frank, why don't you come over for coffee and cake."

"I'd love to," he said with great enthusiasm.

Then I said with my typical straightforwardness, "Frank, may I ask you something? Are you fat?"

He was startled. "What kind of question is that?"

"Are you skinny?"

"No . . . I guess you could say I have a little meat on my bones."

"Wonderful . . . and how tall?"

"About six feet."

"Perfect. Can you come at eleven next Wednesday?"

When the day came, my stomach began to perform a series of flip-flops from the moment I awoke. I said to myself, "What is this pre-date indigestion I'm experiencing? I can't believe it." By ten I was a wreck, and when the doorman rang to announce Frank, I had a desperate urge to go to the bathroom. As I answered the door, I was wiping my dripping palms on the skirt of my dress.

I liked Frank the minute I laid eyes on him. He was a big, nice-looking man, with great warmth radiating from his face. Just exactly as I had imagined him.

"Would you like coffee and cake?" I asked.

"I'd love it," he said, and I liked the way his eyes lit up at the mention of food.

"Small piece or large?"

"Large."

I was smitten.

As we had our coffee and cake, we talked. And I knew that in my life I would never meet anyone else with the magnitude of Frank's intelligence.

"Frank," I said after a while, "tell me why you went to this dating service."

"Oh," he laughed, "because my friends introduce me to the worst people I've ever met. It's funny how our friends think they know what we want, and they don't. They don't really even *know* us—they just know us from when we were married. I decided that maybe a stranger could do a better job."

I was so enthralled with Frank that I became absolutely mute as I listened to him. I know that those of you who have declared my mouth out of bounds will never believe this, but I could hardly speak a word. And as I listened to him talk, my body felt alive.

I asked him about the new woman he'd met and he shook his head sadly. "It didn't work out."

My heart skipped a beat. "What happened?" I asked with an attempt at sympathy.

"We went away for the weekend and it just wasn't what I thought it would be. You see," he said with great seriousness, "my goal is to meet the perfect woman."

"Oh," I snapped without thinking. "You mean the Holy Frail."

"That's funny . . . may I tell you something? You have the most beautiful eyes I've ever seen."

I blushed modestly. "I do?"

He locked me in an intimate stare. "I've traveled all over the world," he said in that rich tone that sent tingles down my spine, "and I have looked into a great many eyes. But I've never seen eyes as beautiful as yours."

Then I got nervous and started thinking, "Oh, God, if anything comes of this relationship, I'm going to have to get up at five every morning to do my face." Because my eyes are just slits. Beige slits. They are not the big beautiful brown eyes they become with makeup. I'm in the class of Rembrandt when it comes to applying makeup.

And then another voice went off in my head and it said, "Virginia, you don't want to get involved with a man again, anyway. What would you do if a man saw you the way you really are?"

I answered the voices in my head: "I'll just have to get up at five in the morning to apply makeup . . . I think it would be worth it."

Finally, Frank said, "This has been such an exciting morning for me. Do you know what I'd like to do? I'd like to make dinner for you next week. I'm a great cook."

We set a date for the following Thursday night. I was absolutely floating, but I was also full of terror. What had I done? What was I getting into?

Now, this might strike you as very extreme behavior, but you must understand that I wasn't in my right mind. The idea of going alone to a man's apartment paralyzed me. So I called my friend and I asked her if she had any plans for Thursday night.

"No, I don't think so."

"Good. Take down this number. Now, you are to call me there every half hour beginning at eight-thirty and you are to say, 'Your package has arrived.' If I respond, 'Open it,' you are to come with the police."

She was delighted to oblige. She hadn't had anything that exciting happen in years.

But then, after all the fuss, I realized I couldn't keep the date. I'd completely forgotten about a previous engagement I had out of town. I called Frank and we arranged for a new date the following Thursday.

I went on my trip and returned and there was no further word from Frank. It was Wednesday and our date was the following evening. I called my friend. "What do you think? Should I call him?"

"Virginia, don't be silly," she said. "Of course you should call him. Ask him when he expects you."

As I was sitting by the phone working up the nerve to do this, it rang. Frank's voice came over the line, but he sounded drawn and distraught.

"Frank, are you all right?" I was alarmed.

"Yes," he answered, but he sounded distracted. "I guess it's the heat."

"Is our date on for tomorrow night?"

"Oh, yes," he replied. But I detected an edge in his voice, so I gallantly said, "Would you rather make it another time? Something sounds wrong."

There was a lengthy pause and then he sighed. "Oh, Virginia, you are so sweet and understanding. You know, I've been waiting all my life to meet the perfect woman, and at last I've found her."

Well, I began to giggle into the phone, a reflex reaction. And what possessed me to be so controlled that upon hearing this news, I didn't gush, "Oh, thank you, I feel the same way," was the most fortunate instinct of my life. Because in the very next breath Frank said, "Virginia, you are just going to love her."

I stopped giggling. "What?"

"She's everything I've always wanted in a woman," he said.

Regaining some control of my voice, I managed to ask, "Is this someone you've just met?"

"No, it's the woman I told you about before."

"Oh. I thought that didn't work out." My voice was now so low that I couldn't even hear it. It was coming right out of my navel.

"It was just an awful misunderstanding. We met again. She came over to my apartment Thursday, and when we looked up, it was Sunday."

I'm not proud of the fact that the next words out of my mouth were, "What did you do for air?" But I was in such a state of shock that I didn't know what I was saying.

Not that I felt I had any claim on Frank. I just couldn't believe that he would sit there and tell me he had spent three days in bed with a woman. And that was how he'd found his Holy Frail.

Before he hung up, Frank said warmly, "Virginia, you'll

never know how much you've meant to me."

And I replied regretfully, "I guess not."

I relate this story not to discourage you about dating services. To the contrary, the fact that I could even meet such a terrific man is a real testimonial to them. In spite of my very real disappointment, I was cheered by the whole experience. It reminded me that I was still a woman, with the deep feelings and longings of a woman.

My biggest mistake was getting my expectations up too high. And after my dating service encounters, I jotted down a few basic rules for you if you go this route. These guidelines will prevent both rip-offs and emotional let-downs.

1. Check with the Better Business Bureau to be sure that the service's credentials are on the up and up.
2. If possible, ask for "testimonials" from satisfied customers in your age and lifestyle range.
3. When you visit a service for the first time, make a note of the physical environment and the kind of people sitting in the waiting room.
4. Shop around before you put your money down. Most services will try to sign you up on your first visit, but don't let them put pressure on you. You want to make the right decision and that takes time and research.
5. Read the contract carefully to learn exactly what it is that the service promises. Some promise only that they will introduce you to a man *if* they find one they think is suitable. Others guarantee a certain number of dates within a specific period.
6. Find out how dates are selected and how rigid the service is about meeting your qualifications.

7. Be sure that the service has customers in your age group. I learned from experience that they don't all deal with older people.

8. Before you join, spend a lot of time thinking about what you want and don't want in a man. Remember that nobody is perfect and no man will fit all of your dream requirements. But get to know the qualities that are really important to you, those things you won't budge on.

9. Also, spend time thinking about what you really want in a relationship. An escort? Companionship? Sex? Marriage? It's important to work that through —*before* you go out on a date—to reduce the unrealistic expectations.

10. Be honest about who *you* are. When you describe yourself and your interests, paint a picture that is accurate. Remember, you don't want a man who doesn't like you as you are.

Some women feel ashamed to use dating services or answer personal ads because they think it's a sign of desperation. That's nonsense. In today's world, it's harder than ever to meet people. It's nothing to be ashamed of that you're interested in having another man in your life.

I'll tell you honestly that dating services are probably not the best route for women over sixty. But if you're under sixty, get up your nerve and give it a try. Like my friend said, what do you have to lose?

I did learn something very important from this experience: Once you expand your mind and stop saying, "Oh, no, I could never do that," you'll be surprised how many new opportunities open themselves up to you.

Find What You're Looking For

Once you've met a man, how do you know if he's right for you? You're probably pretty rusty about these things after many years of marriage. Maybe the only person you have to judge a new man against is your husband. Open your mind to all the wonderful and varied qualities that men have. A second husband doesn't have to be like your first husband. That's the wonderful adventure of life! Variety is the spice.

There are a few sure signs you can look for when you meet a man that will tell you how right he is for you. Take these things into account when you're sizing him up.

1. You have shared interests. The belief that "opposites attract" is pure baloney. There's no magic to chemistry. It's a feeling that evolves from all the things you have in common and enjoy together. When you're older and you don't have children in common, it's especially important that you share the same interests.
2. He treats you with respect. Lack of respect shows up in small ways: a tone of voice he uses, not calling when he says he will, criticizing the way you look or dress. Now that you've achieved a good feeling about yourself, you don't need a man who will tear you down.
3. He doesn't compare you with other women. You don't want a relationship where you're constantly striving to reach the ideals set by another woman. You're a self in your own right. If he doesn't love the self that *you* are, run for your life.
4. He's well groomed. Looks aren't everything, but

grooming certainly can speak volumes about a person. A man who takes care of his grooming is a man who has a secure sense of himself.
5. He puts you first. When you marry, you become the most important person in the other person's life. A man who pays too much attention to what his children think is going to be a troublesome partner. You've got to be number one.

There are other ways of telling if a man is right for you. You know what they are from your own list of personal preferences. Whatever you do, be yourself with a man! Love is a wonderful thing and romance can brighten your life like nothing else. But don't get swept away by the tide of a romance without having your eyes open all of the time.

Have No Shame!

"I think I love Gerald," a friend of mine confided to me one day, her cheeks flushing pink.

"Why, Frieda, that's marvelous," I said enthusiastically. Frieda and Gerald were both widowed. They had been seeing each other for a number of months, and I hadn't seen my friend's eyes sparkle so in a long time.

"When's the wedding?" I teased, but Frieda's brow furrowed in a concerned look.

"We've talked about it," she hedged. "But—"

"But what? You love each other. You're both consenting adults. Go for it."

"Virginia, I know you've been through a lot and you've talked to many people. Is it just me or do other women worry about . . . well . . ."

"Ah." I nodded in sudden understanding. "You're worried about sex."

"Robert was the only one," she said, referring to her deceased husband. "And it's been a long time at that. I'm afraid—"

"Afraid? You're scared to death," I said, laughing. "Perfectly understandable."

If you're like most widows, sex looms as your greatest —and usually unspoken—fear. The thoughts tumbling through your mind follow a course that is something like this:

- "What if I can no longer please a man?"
- "Maybe he'll hate my body."
- "What if he likes things I can't bear to do?"
- "What if I can't adjust to being with a man again?"
- "What if he has problems with impotence?"
- "HELP!"

It may comfort you to know three things. First, there isn't a woman alive, whether she's twenty or sixty, who doesn't have fears like this from time to time. Second, your special concerns as a widow are completely valid. You're not crazy. And third, any woman can have a wonderful sexual relationship again, regardless of her age or how long she was married to her first husband.

Right now you are in a vulnerable position. Since your husband died (and probably before that if he had a long illness) you have been deprived of the kind of loving intimacy you need the most. I don't just mean sex itself, but all the accompanying touching and closeness as well. But you may be embarrassed to admit your need. Maybe you believe that your own longings are like a betrayal of your deceased husband. You might think, "How can I be thinking about myself so selfishly when he is so recently dead?"

Never be ashamed of your need as a woman. The loss of intimacy that you suffered as a result of your husband's death is perhaps the hardest to face and talk about, and the need is real.

When you begin to develop a relationship with a new man, it's quite natural to be worried about what it will be like to be sexual partners. The first thing you should do is lay to rest your past relationship and treat the new one as a completely unique and separate thing. Don't draw comparisons. Don't expect a new man to be like your husband was.

The second thing you should do is *relax*. If two people love each other, they find, almost by instinct, the natural balance that is comfortable and supportive. If you're close enough to have a sexual relationship, you should be close enough to speak honestly about your needs.

Our society's worshipful attitude toward sex has added to our insecurities, especially those of us who are beyond the bloom of youth. And sometimes we forget that physical satisfaction is linked with emotional satisfaction—and that comes from love and caring. Do you really think your new man is going to be appalled by the sight of a little spare tire around your waist? He probably has one too, and he's worrying that *you'll* mind. Chances are, neither of you will care because you'll be too busy loving each other for who you are.

And what about the physical problems that are bound to come with aging? Older people have to contend with a lot of aches and pains and dysfunctions that don't occur among the young, but my advice is to respond to these, too, with an understanding and positive attitude. If arthritis makes one position uncomfortable, try a different one. Be creative. If there is a problem with impotence, don't make a big thing of it. Sexual satisfaction can be achieved in many different ways.

Thank goodness, modern thinking supports the right and ability of men and women to enjoy sex at any age. But I'll bet you harbor a few old notions that you don't need and shouldn't want sex after a certain age. Get them out of your head. Clean out the attic. You're a woman and a sexual being. Go for it!

The Sublime and the Ridiculous

So, now I hope you're beginning to see that you can go out and have a terrific, fulfilling relationship with a man. There are pitfalls along the way, of course—you heard my stories!—but if you keep your sense of humor and your energy for life, you can have everything you want.

The list of ways to meet men is endless. And that's true whether you're forty or seventy. You may prefer to go about the task of finding a man through more traditional channels. But I've heard stories of women who go to outlandish means to get a man. These women possess the gift—and, yes, I believe it is a gift—of being totally up front and assertive about their intentions. No coy game playing whatsoever.

It's like the story of the widow who lived in a Florida condominium. One day she was sunning herself by the pool and she noticed a man she'd never seen before. She walked right up to him and introduced herself. "I've never seen you here before."

"No," he said, "I just moved here."

"You know," she said boldly, "forgive me for saying this, but you look awfully pale. Have you been ill?" He shook his head no.

"Oh, good. You just look like you haven't seen the sun in a while."

"I haven't. I've been in prison."

She was shocked. "Prison! Oh, my! Whatever were you in prison for?"

He looked her straight in the eye and replied, "I bludgeoned my wife to death."

"Oh!" she cried, with joy in her face. "You're single!"

My friends and I laughed so hard over this story, and I don't even think it's true. But the next story is.

I was told of a man whose wife had just died in a nursing home. He was sitting in a room that had one of those transom windows on the door—you know, the top of the door is glass and you can wind it up to let in air or close it. Anyway, his wife had just died the night before and he was sitting with friends. All of a sudden, a huge silver-foil package came flying through the transom. It's a miracle it didn't hit someone. There was a card attached and it read: "Deepest sympathy from a fellow sufferer. Enjoy the pot roast. Tomorrow night, chicken."

As God is my witness, this is a true story.

Then there is the story told to me by a nurse at Mount Sinai Hospital. A woman came to the hospital every day and looked into the waiting room. Finally she went up to the nurse and said, "That man sitting there . . . I know him, but I'm so embarrassed—I can't think of his name."

So the nurse gave her the name.

"Of course. Thank you so much. How's his wife?"

"I'm afraid her condition is critical."

"How sad for him."

Now the woman started going every day and sitting in the waiting room. For the first week she didn't talk to him at all. Finally she said to him one day, "I hope your patient is doing better than mine."

He shook his head. "I'm afraid she's not doing very well at all."

"I'm so sorry to hear that," she replied with great sympathy.

The next day she said to him, "You know, I see you sitting here every day and I don't know what your tastes are, but I make a wonderful coffee cake and I made this for my family. I'd like you to have some for your lunch."

Two days later she brought sandwiches. A week later it was dinner.

His wife died and they were married three months later.

I tell you that there's no limit to the things women will do to meet men. And if you think these stories show incredible nerve, listen to this. A woman from Great Neck, Long Island, went to the house where the family of a deceased woman was receiving after the funeral. She said to the widower, "Leona was such a marvelous woman. We were so close."

And he said, "Yes . . . thank you so much for coming."

"You know," she went on, "one of the things that I really loved about Leona was the way she spoke about you. She used to say that no woman in the world was blessed the way she was to have a husband like you."

"How nice. What did you say your name was?"

"Marjorie Smith."

"Have we ever met before?"

"No, I don't believe we have."

He was puzzled. "That's funny. I don't recall Leona ever mentioning your name."

"Oh, we worked together at the hospital and on charity work . . ."

Eventually they were married. And Marjorie will go to her grave with the secret that she had never met Leona in her life.

Shed Your Fears

Finally, I want to tell you to give up your fear of rejection. It will hold you back. A lot of you think that if a man you like is not also attracted to you, that means there's something wrong with you. Get it out of your head that it's *you*. Maybe you're just not right for each other. Think back to the time before you were married. How many men did you date before you met your husband? You're back on the same merry-go-round now. Don't ever feel invalidated as a person because the chemistry between you and a man isn't right.

If I had a deep fear of rejection, I know I never would have opened myself up to many of the wild and wonderful experiences I've had during the past few years. Even as I write this, I've met a man that I like. And I'm not going to hide out in my apartment because I'm afraid of rejection. Not on your life!

I met this man at a party and I was so attracted to him. He was nice looking, sophisticated, funny. He had a wonderful sense of humor. Well, I really admire a man with a brain and humor, and I wasn't ashamed to tell my hostess, "I find him very attractive. Tell me about him."

She clapped her hands with delight and cried, "Hooray! There's life in the old girl yet."

So, do you know what I'm going to do? I'm going to have a dinner party and invite him to come. Because I must tell you honestly, before I go off to that big ballroom in the sky, I would like to have a man in my life again. And I know that it's up to me to go out there and find him.

◈ 3 ◈

Let the Widow Beware!

———

When my friend Judith told me that she was going to attend a séance to communicate with her dead husband, I just shook my head. What next?

I tried to reason with her, especially when she let me in on the price tag on this phone call to the Other World. "Judith," I said, "these people just prey on widows. It's a scam. There's no way you're going to get through to Ed."

"Well, I believe it," she huffed.

"He's gone, dear," I said gently. "It's time for you to get on with your life and say good-bye to him . . ."

Judith gave me a withering look. "Don't you think I know that? I'm not trying to bring him back. I just have some unfinished business with him, that's all. One little chat should take care of it."

There was an awful gleam in her eye as she said this,

and I asked cautiously, "What exactly is it you want to say to Ed?"

"Come with me and find out for yourself," she said abruptly. And I agreed. I wouldn't miss *this* one for the world!

Judith had found a woman in New York who, she said, "guaranteed to get you through to the loved one of your choice." We called and signed up for a session.

Now, before the actual event, they required us to go through a training session to learn séance etiquette. This session was presided over by an assistant who was a real battle-ax of a woman. She reminded me of a sergeant in boot camp.

There were eight of us in the group, and she seated us around an oval table and told us to clasp hands. "Please tell no one your last name," she instructed. "We will use first names only."

We grabbed hands and sat perfectly still, waiting for further instructions.

"Now," said the drill sergeant, "repeat after me in unison: 'We hope it's a favorable night.'"

"We hope it's a favorable night," we chorused.

"Very good. Now say, 'We will be very happy to talk to a loved one.'"

"We will be very happy to talk to a loved one."

"We will not say anything that will cause distress to a loved one." I glanced at Judith and saw that she was repeating this line with clenched teeth and I thought, "Uh oh, we're in for some trouble here."

"Now," said our instructor, "we will all come to the evening without eating."

I interrupted. "Why? Are you afraid someone will belch and drive the spirits away?"

"No comments from anyone," she said sternly, shooting

me a disapproving look. "You will not have any gum in your mouth . . ."

I repeated, "We will not have any gum—"

"No," she snapped. "You don't have to repeat that." It was becoming apparent to her that I wasn't the average docile participant, and I could tell she wasn't too happy to have me there.

We passed our training with flying colors, in spite of me, and were told to return the following evening for the real thing. As we left the building, I began to laugh and Judith glared at me. "If that's your attitude, I don't think you should come."

My eyes widened in mock horror. "Are you kidding? I wouldn't miss this for the world. I'm just dying to hear what you have to say to Ed."

When we arrived the following evening, we were shown into a dim, candlelit room. Our drill sergeant from the previous evening seated us around the table. When we had settled into our seats and were clasping hands, she began to speak in a hushed voice. "You must open yourselves up to the spirit," she said. "And the spirit takes many forms. Perhaps you will see a wisp of light floating through the air and that light will touch you. If the spirit touches you, you are to say, 'Thank you. I have been touched.' Now, repeat it after me."

I said, "Thank you, I am touched."

"No, no, that's not what I said. I said, 'I have been touched.'"

I pointed to my head. "I think I *am* touched to be here in the first place."

She was furious with me, but she kept her voice low. "We must have no dissenting voices in the group. This is no place for anyone who does not wish to communicate." I rearranged my face into the proper solemnity. "I'm sorry."

"Then," she continued, "you may hear a voice calling your name. And if you hear your name being called, you are to reply, 'I'm here . . . I'm here.'"

At last we were ready, and the room took on a reverent hush as the curtains parted and our medium walked in. She was fully decked out in robe and turban, and on her face was the entire contents of the Bloomingdale's makeup department. The paint was so thick that it was impossible to tell whether she was twenty or eighty. She was also carrying a wand, which I thought was a particularly nice touch.

For those of you who are not familiar with séances, let me explain here that the medium does not actually speak directly to the spirits herself. She acts through an invisible assistant, kind of a cosmic telephone operator who makes the connection and sees that you're put through to the right party. Our medium's assistant was a floating spirit named Reindeer.

She began to call him. "Reindeer . . . Reindeer . . ."

I glanced over at Judith and saw that she looked very pale in the flickering candlelight. "Do you want to leave?" I whispered.

She tightened her lips. "No."

I also noticed that everyone around the table was frozen in attention. They were all very intense as they waited to speak to their departed loved ones. I knew it was hopeless ever to imagine that I could get through to Harry. He wouldn't have come to a party like this when he was alive and he certainly wasn't going to show up now.

"Reindeer . . . Reindeer . . . ," our leader was calling, swaying back and forth in her seat. "Is there anyone who wants to speak with us, Reindeer?"

And suddenly a voice boomed out of the ceiling. "Yes, there is."

The leader looked around the table with a smugly satisfied smile. "Do you all hear Reindeer's voice?"

We nodded, and I mused that the quality of the cassette seemed excellent.

Reindeer's voice boomed out again. "Judith . . . Judith . . ."

My friend sprang to life, digging her nails into my palm. "I'm here! I'm here!"

"Someone wants to speak with you, Judith."

"Put him through! Put him through!" Judith was yelling.

"Edward wants to speak with you, Judith."

"Well, I want to speak with him," Judith's voice was strident.

And now we heard another voice, faint and whispery. It certainly could not be identified as Ed's voice . . . or anyone else's, for that matter. "Judith . . . Judith . . ."

"Ed, is that you?" cried Judith. "Speak up, I can't hear you."

"Judith . . . Judith . . ."

"Listen, Ed, this is important. Where did you put the insurance policies? I've looked everywhere. I've torn the house apart. What is this, some kind of cruel joke?"

"Judith . . . ," the whispery voice called. "I can't hear you."

"Don't give me that," Judith sputtered. "This call is costing me a fortune and I want an answer. How can you rest in peace when you know your poor wife is down here practically starving to death?"

Everyone at the table was staring at Judith, transfixed, and I grabbed her arm and shook it. "Judith, come on," I cajoled. "Say good-bye to Ed. Come on, let's end it now."

She wrenched her arm away. "No," she hissed. "I paid

for this and I'm not leaving until I know where those damn policies are."

But the medium, who had been observing this disruptive scene in silent fury, stepped in and raised her hand. The whispering voice of Ed disappeared into thin air. "There are some very disturbing elements in this room and I think we're going to have to dispel them before we can continue," declared the medium, fixing a hard look on Judith and me.

The drill sergeant appeared from nowhere and we were firmly escorted from the room, Judith calling back demands to be given a complete refund of her money. By the time we hit the street, I was laughing so hard that tears were running down my cheeks. "Judith," I gasped, "you're a damn fool."

Judith's cheeks were flushed bright red with indignation. "Well, I'm goddamned mad. That woman ripped me off."

I gently took her arm and propelled her down the street. "Let's go eat. I'm starving."

"But she—"

"She ripped you off." I nodded. "Tomorrow I'll come over and help you look for the insurance policies."

I relate this story as an example of how easy it is to get taken advantage of when you're a widow . . . especially if you were very dependent on your husband and never learned how to maneuver in the world on your own. I'm not even saying that all psychics are rip-offs because I'm something of a believer in psychic phenomena. But clearly Judith's experience fell into a very questionable category. With all due respect to Reindeer . . .

When the man you loved and lived with for most of

your adult life passes away, you *want* to believe he's not really gone. With all your heart you want to believe it. And when someone tells you very convincingly that, yes, it is possible to speak to him again, your judgment can be clouded by the sheer power of your hope. I saw a television program recently that demonstrated the most outrageous example of this. It really made me laugh. A woman had built a business where she sent messages to loved ones beyond the grave. And do you know how she did it? She took the messages to terminally ill patients in hospitals and paid them to memorize the messages so they could deliver them when they got to the other side. She charged her customers—mostly grieving widows—$2,500 per message.

You may be the toughest woman in the world, smart and savvy and independent. But in the face of your husband's death, you may have found many of your old reserves crumbling. I know that happened to me. I was always very strong and I prided myself on my wisdom about the world. But in the months following Harry's death I lived in a dizzy state of unreality. My legendary strength and good judgment had flown out the window. It's a vulnerable time . . . and there are a lot of people out there who know how vulnerable you are and won't think twice about taking advantage of you.

Scams Abound

My friend Hilda called me one day sounding very excited. Hilda's husband of thirty years had died about five months earlier and it was good to hear her sound so perky. "Virginia," she said excitedly, "I'm going on a trip."

"That's great, Hilda," I replied enthusiastically. "You could use one. Where are you going?"

"Well, first I'm going to Florida for a few days and then I'm going on a week-long cruise to the Bahamas."

"Really." I hesitated for a moment, then said cautiously, "Um, Hilda, I know you've been having some money problems... have you come into some money?"

"No," she gushed. "That's the wonderful thing about it. The whole trip is free... or practically free."

"What on earth are you talking about?" I had never heard anything like this before.

"It all started when I got this card in the mail saying I'd won this trip. I was suspicious, of course. But when I called them I found it was all on the up and up. It's a deal sponsored by this real estate development company in Florida. All I have to do is go look at some land while I'm there and it qualifies me for the trip. I was computer selected."

"Hilda," I said doubtfully.

"It's not a bad idea because I was thinking maybe I'd move to Florida, anyway."

"You were?"

"Sure, why not? So I sent in my deposit—"

"I thought you said it was free."

"It is. Except for the three-hundred-dollar deposit to show I'm serious. I'll get it back."

"Hilda," I said evenly, "have you ever heard the expression 'I smell a rat'?"

A month later Hilda left on her Florida trip. "It was okay," she reported upon her return. "The accommodations could have been nicer, but what the heck. The best part of this deal is the cruise, anyway."

Need I tell you that Hilda never took her cruise? Nor

did she ever receive her deposit back. In fact, the firm that awarded Hilda this remarkable prize mysteriously disappeared off the face of the earth. The upshot was that Hilda spent $300 for a miserable four days in Orlando. It could have been worse.

I am an optimistic soul, but generally I abide by one rule: *If it sounds too good to be true, it's too good to be true.*

There isn't a punishment great enough for those people who prey on lonely, insecure women—especially widows. But it's useless to pretend that these scams don't exist, and you should be prepared for them.

Within weeks after Harry's death I was barraged, through the mail and over the phone, by real estate brokers, accountants, lawyers, insurance companies, loan companies and investment companies.

The grapevine works very fast. And when word gets out that you're "in transition," watch out!

You may be thinking, "With all the things on my mind right now, how am I going to be sharp enough to avoid rip-offs?"

My first piece of advice is that you must not depend entirely on yourself. Have a lawyer and an accountant. Refer all requests to them. Period. Stay uninvolved. Or if you can't do that, at least make it clear whenever anyone calls you that you have other people to check with. Say, "I'd better discuss this with my son, who is the captain of the police department." Whatever works. If you appear not to be vulnerable—surprise! You're *not* vulnerable.

Decisions, Decisions

When you become a widow, there are a million decisions that suddenly have to be made, and if you're like me, you might feel lacking in what it takes to make them. Throughout my marriage I happily let Harry handle all the arrangements, from balancing the checkbook to purchasing the furniture. I had no head for that kind of thing and he did. He knew how to find a bargain better than anyone. Practical decisions came easily to him, while I tended to hem and haw and be indecisive.

After Harry died I looked around the apartment we had lived in for twenty years and I said, "I just can't bear to live here anymore. I'm going to move."

Easy to say.

Having made that decision, I didn't have the vaguest idea what to do. My mind buzzed with questions: How do I sell the apartment? What price should I ask? Should I call a broker? How do I know which broker is good? What kind of place should I buy? Will I end up losing all my money? What if I sell before I buy?

I was aware of the potential for disaster in such a move and I nearly gave up the whole idea. It seemed too overwhelming. But it was during that experience that I learned an essential lesson that has seen me through all my traumatic decisions since that time.

Just as I was getting ready to reach for the telephone book to look up real estate brokers, a thought crossed my mind. "Why don't I give Steve a call?" Steve and his wife, Emily, were a couple who lived in my building and we were pretty friendly. I explained my dilemma to Steve, who recommended a reputable company, and I was off and running.

Don't forget: No matter who you are, *you know somebody.* And that somebody knows somebody else, and that somebody . . . you get the picture. Stay away from the Yellow Pages when you're trying to make a decision. Ask a friend. Ask a neighbor. Ask the nice man at your bank.

Or the receptionist at your beauty parlor. Expand your personal services network by utilizing the people who are your greatest resource.

Let me suggest a little exercise. It's something I did myself several months after Harry died. A psychologist suggested it to me and it worked, so I'll pass it along to you.

Take a sheet of paper and at the top write: "My New Life."

Then, list all the things you have to take care of. These should be practical items, not emotional ones, like changing your residence. Your list might include things like this:

1. Sell house
2. Move into apartment
3. Change bank accounts
4. Change insurance policies
5. Put furniture in storage
6. Write new will
7. Create a budget

It will probably be a long list. In fact, you're going to immediately get discouraged about how many things there are to take care of. You might find yourself grumbling as I did, "Nobody ever told me that widowhood is a full-time job."

But hang in there. Once you've completed your list of all the things you have to take care of, write at least one name after each item on the list. These names make up your adviser panel. They can be anybody whom you trust enough to ask questions of.

Performing this exercise gave me a new sense of power. I said to myself, "You're not alone! You have all these people you can call on for advice." It's a very good feeling.

Now, I can hear your mind working. You're thinking, "Oh, they wouldn't want to be bothered with my silly little questions." Sure they would. People love to be asked their advice. They love to be asked if they know experts. They love it, they love it, they love it. Most likely, you've performed kindnesses for these same people over the years. How did it make *you* feel to do them favors? Pretty good, I would imagine. Well, that's exactly the way they're going to feel doing you favors.

The point is, you're alone now and maybe it's the first time in your life that you've ever been alone. Have a healthy respect for your weakness, as well as for your strength. Understand that you need other people just as much as you always did. And accept without shame the gifts of counsel that your friends give you.

Protect Yourself

I hadn't seen Irene at the beauty parlor since her husband passed away two months earlier. "Isn't it about time Irene started getting out and about?" I asked a mutual friend.

"I don't know. She was pretty broken up when Irv died. And remember, Irene isn't the healthiest person in the world herself."

"I'm going to call her," I said. "I want to be sure she's okay."

When I got Irene on the phone, she sounded down.

"We all miss you," I told her. "When are you coming back?"

"My arthritis has been acting up a little," she said, hedging.

"Irene, cut it out," I said bluntly. "I've known you for many years and it isn't like you to hide in your house. What's going on?"

"Okay," she sighed. "A woman in my building got mugged last month—right out in front in the full light of day. They took her purse and knocked her down."

"So? Has it escaped your notice for twenty years that you live in New York City?" I asked.

"Virginia, it could happen to me . . . I couldn't move fast enough to . . . those gangs that roam the streets . . . they're just looking for—"

"Whoa! Irene, you're being irrational. You've lived in this city all your life and I've never known you to be a nervous Nelly."

"I'm not as young as I used to be," she replied primly.

"Well, who is?" I laughed. "Listen, I know you're feeling a little shaky now that you don't have a man around the house. When Harry died I thought every creak of a floorboard was a psychotic attacker coming to do me in. But part of living is going out, so you've got to find a way around this. I'll tell you what, next week I'll come by in a taxi and we'll go to the beauty parlor together."

And that's what we did. Eventually Irene began to feel secure enough to go out on her own. The first time I ran into her on the street I was delighted. Irene had come through the dark fears.

I'm not playing down the fact that the fears are real. An older woman alone is considered to be an easy target. But there are ways of protecting yourself. Here are a few of my ideas about that, learned from eight years of widowhood:

1. Establish a network of your single friends. Do things together. Travel in pairs or groups. Not only

is this safer but it's also more fun than going places alone. To carry this idea one step further, I know a group of five women who call each other every day, once in the morning and once in the evening, to make sure that each woman in the group is okay. Isn't that a lovely idea?

2. Make sure your house or apartment is secure and has an operating alarm system. If the locks on your doors haven't been changed for eons, have them checked out. Police authorities inform me that the older models of locks are unsafe. Speak to your locksmith about the newer, sturdier locks, like the Medeco, which is virtually pick-proof.

3. If you frequently have items delivered from the grocery, familiarize yourself with the delivery personnel and let the store manager know that you're concerned about safety. Never release the chain on your door until you're certain it's the person you're expecting. If you don't know the delivery boy, have him leave the groceries outside the door and don't open it until he leaves.

4. Wear comfortable, low heels when you're walking on the street. Don't go hobbling along in your high heels. They make you look vulnerable and you are. You want to have some sense of mobility.

5. Don't wear expensive jewelry on the street. Don't even wear jewelry that *looks* expensive. Pocket it until you reach your destination.

6. When you're in a taxi or car at night, insist that you be taken to your door and ask the driver to wait until he can see that you're safely inside.

7. This sounds cruel, but *ignore* any cries for help on the street. I hate to say it, but too often the people who rush up to you in "dire need" are part of a

scam to distract you so that your purse can be stolen. It's such a sad fact of modern society that we have to turn our backs in this way. But put your own safety first.

8. Make friends with all the storekeepers in your neighborhood. If they know you, they will form an invisible protection squad.

9. Vary your schedule and your route. Don't be completely predictable. (Ugh! Who wants to be predictable anyway?)

10. Look like you're someone to be reckoned with. Attitude plays an important role in safety, and that's why older women are the easiest targets. They don't have attitude. Get some. If you walk down the street like a victim, you're more likely to become a victim. If you walk down the street like a black belt in karate, nobody will touch you.

11. Finally, your best protection when you're alone is not to be alone. Be a person who is surrounded by people . . . from friends to shopkeepers. Earn a reputation as someone who lives inside a tight shell of protection formed by the people you love.

When You Get the Willies

When Harry died I was used to being an independent person who could operate in the world. It was the nights that got me. When I finally turned off the T.V. and the noises outside my window had died down, I got the willies! This will strike you as ridiculous (or, on second thought, maybe it won't), but every single night I would not be able to go to bed until I had gone through the following routine: I had to look under the bed for ax murderers; check in every closet for ghosts; stick my head in every single kitchen cabinet and under the sink for mice, rats, snakes and monsters of undetermined origin; check behind the shower curtain—shades of *Psycho;* call the number for Time so I could hear a human voice; call the number for Weather so I could hear another human voice; lie on the floor by my door and peer out the crack to be sure no one was standing there.

It's a wonder I ever got any sleep!

After I had been religiously going through this routine for some time, I mentioned it one day to a friend who was involved in yoga.

"I have an alternative," she said, smiling. "Before you go to sleep, lie on your bed in the dark—or you might want to burn a scented candle. Close your eyes and begin to take long deep breaths... in through your nose, out through your mouth. Clear your mind and concentrate on relaxing every tiny part of your body. When you are completely relaxed and feel a gentle tingling in your limbs, imagine a beautiful calm scene—a grassy field or a blue sky filled with puffy clouds... "

Armed with this new weapon against the willies, I went home and that night I tried it. I was asleep long before I got to the puffy clouds. And I haven't had the willies since.

Fear, my friends, is a state of mind. If you are secure, happy, alert and savvy, no person or thing is going to have power over you.

◈ *4* ◈

Family Traps

"It isn't just that I was Ben's wife," Edith reminded me. "I was . . . am . . . the mother of his children."

"Of course," I agreed. "What's your point?"

She shook her head, frustrated by a complexity I couldn't quite see. "Now that Ben is gone I have a lot to deal with. Not only my own life, but theirs as well."

I chose my words carefully, but they still seemed harsh. "The last time I checked, your son, Peter, was forty-one and Joan was thirty-six. In my book, that qualifies as adulthood."

"They're both very traumatized by their father's death."

"Of course."

"And I feel responsible for them."

I saw a sudden light. "Edith, is there something you're not saying?"

She hesitated for a moment before admitting in a rush of words, "I really want to support them, and God knows I want them to always know how much I loved their father and how sad I am to be without him, but . . ." Her voice trailed off.

"But?"

She sighed. "I have to get on with things."

"Of course," I said again.

"They don't quite see it that way."

"What happened?" I suspected there was a reason behind this outpouring.

"I had a date," she said miserably.

"Really?" This was something I could sink my teeth into. "So, what's the problem? Given that the statistics of older women even coming within five miles of a man are so grim, I'd think you'd be jumping for joy."

"Well, I was, originally. I was really quite thrilled. It's been hard for me, and now I figured, okay, this is great, I'm getting on with my life. I'm only sixty-two, after all. But when I mentioned it to Joan, she acted very odd."

"What did she say?"

"She meant well." Edith was determined to defend her daughter. "But, I don't know . . . there was something in her voice that didn't ring right. She was very stiff about it. And later Peter called. Apparently she had called him right away. He was livid . . . *livid.*"

"Livid?" I repeated dumbly. I didn't quite understand.

"He felt I was transgressing some line of propriety."

"You?" I laughed. Edith was the queen of propriety, the matron of social exactitude. She had never transgressed a line in her life.

"He said very plainly, 'Mother, it's only been eight months—how could you?'"

"And you said..." This was like a soap opera. I was enthralled.

"I said I'd call him back later."

"What?" I was appalled. "You didn't defend yourself?"

"What could I say?" She shrugged hopelessly. "He wasn't going to listen to reason. Ben and Peter were always very close."

"The question is," I said, "did you go on the date?"

Her eyes sparkled. "I sure did. I had fun, too. But I guess it's best that the children don't know."

I burst out laughing. "Really, Edith, this is too funny. Here you are, sixty-two years old and you're sneaking out on dates behind your children's backs."

"I know," she grimaced. "When I think back to the trouble I had with Joan in that department, I really just shake my head. Sometimes I wonder who the parent is here."

Ah, I thought later, that's an excellent question. Something very peculiar happens to the relationship between a widow and her children. You could be the most powerful, independent woman in the world, then suddenly you're a widow and... *bang!* Your children start treating you like a five-year-old child with an advanced case of senility. It's a fact.

My friend Barbara had a similar story. "It just makes me uncomfortable the way my son Paul calls me twice a day," she confided. "I love to hear from him, but this is ridiculous. When his father was alive, we were lucky if we heard from him twice a month. I'm grateful that he's concerned, but to tell you the truth, I just wish he'd let me breathe. He keeps making noises about my moving in with him and it's the last thing in the world I'd ever want to do."

The relationship between a mother and her adult children, precarious under the best of circumstances, is twice as hard when the woman becomes widowed. The death of a significant member of the family brings the mother and children together in a special way. Their bond during the grieving period is stronger than ever. But after a time the bond can grow claustrophobic and nobody knows quite how to let go. When a widow begins to live a normal life on her own, it's a message to the children that she's declaring an end to the old life, the life she shared with their father. They react in various ways to this news. Often their reaction is to indicate that she is betraying a man who is no longer alive. And the widow is consumed with greater guilt at a time when she's already struggling for a balance. It can be a big mess.

I have to admit it's a very delicate matter—especially when you decide to start dating men. Even the most mature children are going to have a problem with this.

My friend Paula told me how her daughter tried to sabotage every effort she made to meet men . . . all, of course, "in the best interests" of her mother.

"She knew I was seeing Greg. I didn't keep it a secret. After about two months she made a point of inviting us both to dinner at her house. I thought it was a lovely gesture, but I should have known better.

"From the moment we arrived, she gave him a hard time. Greg is seventy-five and he has a bit of a hearing problem, so her barrage of questions was tough for him to deal with. I was really embarrassed. Later my daughter pulled me into the kitchen and gave me a big lecture. 'He's so *old*,' she said. 'You can do better than that.' I told her that Greg and I had a good time together and I didn't really care about how old he was. I'm not exactly a spring chicken myself!

"Then came the final blow. She had the *nerve* to ask me if we were . . . *intimate.* I was completely humiliated, and I had to control myself not to just slap her in the face. I told her it was none of her business. We haven't spoken since."

Sometimes the children of a widow want her to act exactly as she did when they were growing up. They want everything to freeze. They can't face that you're a new person now. And then you may go along with them to keep the peace, but secretly you're resentful.

You think, "Where are they when I'm lying there at night, overcome with loneliness? Where are they on those long weekends when I haven't a thing in the world to do and the phone never rings? Where are they when I yearn to have another human being around who's my own age, someone I can relate to, someone who can appreciate me and maybe give me a hug when I'm feeling down? *How dare they criticize me for the small efforts I'm making to be happy?*"

Every widow goes through this adjustment with her children, and you're no different. You *must* sit down with them and talk this through. Lay it on the line. Say to them, "I want you to stop thinking of me as the widow of your father and start thinking of me as a single woman with a life of my own." Be gentle. Say, "You know how much I loved your father and I will always love him. But it's time to let go."

If they react negatively, *insist.* I know how hard it is to go against the grain in this respect. But children are lovable creatures who can become complete bullies if given the chance. Refuse to let them.

Be sympathetic to their pain, but don't let your sympathy get the better of you. Recognize their fear that when you begin to move on in your life, it's a signal that their father is *really* dead. You may say, "But he *is* really dead." That's true, but it doesn't always sink in emotionally until your children see you on the arm of another man. And suddenly they have a whole new series of adjustments to make.

I was chatting one day with a taxi driver who told me how much he admired his mother for the wonderful job she did raising her children after her husband died.

I asked him, "How long ago did your father die?" and he said, "Thirty years ago."

I was surprised. "Didn't she ever remarry?" I asked.

"Oh, no," he said. "She had to raise us first. She wouldn't have brought a stranger into the house."

I thought to myself, "What a foolish woman." Because now her children are all grown and she's alone. The taxi driver mentioned how worried he was about her now because she seemed so lonely.

The expression "life goes on" seems harsh, but it's true. You must demand personal freedom from your children. And make it stick.

"Why Don't You Call?"

Of course, the reverse is also true. Many women find themselves falling into the nagging mother routine, clinging to their children as to a lifeboat in a stormy sea.

There's a great joke: A priest, a minister and a rabbi were arguing about when life really begins. The priest said, "Life begins at conception." The minister disagreed. "No, life begins at birth." The rabbi shook his head and said, "You're both wrong. In our religion we believe that life begins when the children leave the house and the dog runs away."

Maybe you always looked forward to the time when your children would grow up, get married and lead lives of their own. But now you're a widow, and suddenly the tables have turned and you're complaining that they never call you. Your children love you. Being a widow does not entitle you to become a burden to them.

A woman I know recently made all kinds of cutting comments about her daughter and then complained to me, "Alice doesn't even know I'm alive."

I said to her, "Oh, she knows you're alive, all right! No dead person could possibly be full of as much venom as you are."

Make it a joy for your children to call you. Don't carry on about being lonely and neglected. My own mother was like that. No matter when I called her, it was always the wrong time. She'd say, "I wish you had called me yesterday. I felt marvelous." Finally I was so exasperated that I said, "Okay, you're right. From now on, I'm only going to call you yesterday."

I know women who are determined to make their children feel guilty just for living. They'll call and say, "What are you doing tonight?" Upon hearing the plans, they'll say, with the barest hint of a whine, "Oh, that's so nice that you and Ted are going out to dinner . . . I guess I'll just fix myself a little soup and try to entertain myself *alone*."

Fishing for invitations under these circumstances is humiliating and belittling. Allow your children their freedom. Get the chip off your shoulder. If you're an interesting, vibrant person to be around, they will want to be around you. Period.

It's best to set the terms of your new relationship as soon as possible after your husband dies. Make it clear that you don't expect them to drop everything to take care of you. If their custom was to come to dinner once a week, keep it once a week. Don't demand all their attention—they have their own lives to lead and so do you!

The Ten Rules

I have created ten rules for relating to your children as a widow. Post them on your wall. Refer to them every day. Memorize them. Give your children a copy too, to let them know where you stand.

1. Don't say to your children, "You remember me, don't you?" Whining is very unattractive. What purpose is served by heaping guilt on your children? They may not react overtly, but you can bet they'll resent you privately. Sure, you brought them into the world, but that doesn't give you any rights. They have to find their own way, just as you do.

2. If your children criticize your behavior, remind them of when they were younger. Say, "When I used to try to tell you what to do, you said, 'Oh, Mom, mind your own business.' And I'm saying to you now, mind your own business." Sometimes children feel as if they've become your parent. It's a senseless role reversal and it won't happen if you refuse to tolerate it.

3. Discuss the way things are going to be now that you're a widow. Take your children into your confidence. Explain to them why the changes you're making are so important. They'll appreciate the

fact that you trust them enough to level with them.

4. Include your children in your important decisions, but make it clear that the final decision is yours, not theirs. I'm not telling you that the children shouldn't play an important part in your life, but, finally, you're the one who has to live with you, not them.

5. Don't allow yourself to be bullied into choices you don't really want to make. You're very vulnerable right now and it might be easy just to go along with what is suggested. But take the time to examine your own feelings and needs before you make any big decisions.

6. Never move in with your children unless it is absolutely necessary. The umbilical cord was cut long ago. This is not a good time to retie it.

7. Make your relationships with men off limits to the opinions of your children. It's a personal matter between you and the man, and they have no say. They wouldn't tolerate your interference in their relationships, so why should you tolerate theirs?

8. If you need legal, financial or medical advice, don't go to your children for it. Establish independence in the way you handle your affairs.

9. Don't depend on your children for your social life. It will hamper your ability to meet new people. Some widows never go out unless their children invite them. This is not healthy. You need to spend time with people your own age.

10. Be the person you always were with them—that longtime loving, caring, giving woman. But keep the distance required to find your own way in life.

Handling Other Relatives

Of course, it's not just your children you have to consider. Chances are, you have a whole barrel full of miscellaneous relations to deal with. Your family can be the most important support system you have. It can also be an oppressive, confusing tangle. When your husband was alive, it was probably simple to relate to everyone. You established a pattern and that was that. Now you have to rebuild those relationships on a different footing. It takes love and patience.

HIS RELATIONS

Chances are, the family is supportive of you. But some widows find that their husband's relatives become cool to them after he's gone. As one woman observed in a puzzled manner, "I almost feel as though George's sister blames me because she thinks I didn't take good enough care of him. When I'm around her, I feel like such a failure. She'd probably like to do a switch and put *me* in the grave."

As much as your husband's family may have grown to love you over the years, you may find this a tense time to be around them. The primary reason for your relationship—your husband—is gone, and maybe they're uncertain about how to relate to you. Should they try to fill his shoes somehow, calling you every day? Should they leave you alone? Should they wait for you to make the first move? Don't blame them if they're uncomfortable. They have their own grief to deal with too. My suggestion is that you be as natural with them as always. And make a special effort to keep the lines of communication open. It's too easy to let the relationships of a lifetime crumble with neglect.

YOUR SIBLINGS

I know a woman who has literally been terrorized by her older brother, an accountant, ever since her husband died.

"He's having the time of his life figuring out how I'm going to spend the rest of *my* life," she told me bitterly. "Every time I make a move, I get a two-hour lecture about how I made the wrong choice."

"Have you told him how you feel?"

"I've tried, but he's my only brother and he feels responsible. Virginia, I'm considering having my number changed and making it unlisted. Every time the phone rings, I get a sinking feeling."

"He loves you," I observed. "For starters."

"I know . . . but I saw him pull the same routine on Mother before she died, and I can't stand the thought of having him looking over my shoulder. I'm hardly a helpless young girl."

"Hardly," I agreed. My friend was a beautiful, self-possessed woman who owned her own business and was accustomed to her independence. "Why don't you call him and set up a meeting? Lay down the law."

That's what she did, too, and she reports that he's "better," but it's still an uphill battle.

Especially if you only have one or two siblings, they'll probably become amazingly protective of you in the period following your husband's death. At first that may come as a relief. You won't mind being taken care of. But eventually, you're not going to want it anymore and they might be reluctant to give up the role.

You must establish the ground rules from the start. Tell them, "I love you and I'm grateful for your kindness and support. It's nice to know you're there if I need you. But it's important for me to handle things on my own, too, now that I'm alone. In fact, the idea of developing self-sufficiency is exciting for me. It's what helps me get by, and you can love me the most by letting me find my way."

GRANDCHILDREN

My grandchildren are the most wonderful treasures in my life. We have a very close relationship. They were very dear to Harry when he was alive and they miss him. But they don't try to control my life—younger people aren't as prone to that behavior.

If your grandchildren are very young when your husband dies, they may be filled with questions about what happened to their grandfather. You may not want to deal with them directly, but try to be patient and answer their questions. Allow them the freedom to mourn. And be as honest as possible. Young people are very quick to recognize dishonesty.

Another thing to remember about your grandchildren is that they have lives of their own. I love it when Jan and Stephen want to spend time with me, but I never push them. I know they love me, but I don't expect them to be my buddies. They have their friends and their busy lives and I know it's important not to interfere.

Your family is your most precious resource, and it's a wonderful thing to know that you have people who are there for you through thick and thin. But no one can fill the empty places inside you. You have to do that yourself. It takes courage to establish an independent life. But you must do it . . . for your sake and for theirs.

◈ 5 ◈

Thank God I'm Two-Faced

I have always said that I'm glad to be two-faced. I maintain that the face I wake up with in the morning isn't the one I necessarily have to wear all day. I am a great believer in the power of makeup and I can rival Rembrandt in the ability to use paint.

But the issue of beauty and fashion goes deeper than slapping a little paint on the face. I've found that when I'm feeling my most vulnerable and insecure, the confidence gained from looking my best can really boost my spirits.

Is this superficial? Sure. But so what? Anything you can do to make yourself glow in the harsh light of the world is worth the effort. And right now, when you're struggling to get on your feet again and recover your self-esteem, physical attractiveness is important.

If you've seen me on television, you know that I always have my hair coiffed, wear plenty of makeup, and have long fire-engine-red nails. I go in for the dramatic packaging. That's me, not necessarily you. But looking good—whatever your personal style—is important. And don't pooh-pooh this by saying, "It makes sense for Virginia. She's in the public eye. It's not so important for me to look great all the time." Let me tell you something about that. You *are* in the public eye. I have to look at you!

I remember a little verse from my youth that goes like this:

> *I know I ain't no shining star,*
> *I know how ugly my face are,*
> *But I don't mind it*
> *Cuz I hide behind it,*
> *It's folks outside that gets the jar.*

I may get into trouble for saying this, but I don't care. There is absolutely no excuse for a woman to be homely. I wonder at the conceit of a woman who thinks she can get up in the morning and go outside looking the way some women look on the street. Do these women live in homes without mirrors? I see women who look inexcusably bad. And it's usually nothing that a little makeup and a decent hairstyle wouldn't take care of. I believe we have a responsibility to the people around us to look our best.

Maybe you're feeling sorry for yourself and thinking, the way I did when Harry died, that it's too late to make a difference. You tell yourself, "My life is over and I think I'll just slink off into frumpy old age." *Nonsense.* You're living a new phase of your life. And you're probably overdue for an overhaul. Maybe when your husband was alive he would not allow you to get your hair cut a certain way or wear the kind of clothes you really liked. But you're on your own now and maybe for the first time in your life you can really experiment with looking the way that makes you feel special.

So let me share a few of my thoughts about how you can achieve your best and most vibrant look—the look that will carry you through the new adventures in your life.

Jane Fonda I'm Not

Having said all this, I must tell you that in this age of the "body beautiful" it's like a mine field out there. Don't take the idea of beauty too seriously or you'll be crushed in the tide of exercise mania. The most fit and lovely fifty-year-old woman can feel like a Milk Dud in the company of true fitness fanatics.

For example, one thing that really aggravates me is the commercials they have on television advertising the exercise studios. They show a group of slender women in leotards, and set among them like a beached whale is a fat woman.

That's an insult. There is nothing as humiliating as being the only fat woman in an exercise class. What woman in her right mind would subject herself to this humiliation? I wish there were more exercise classes for women who wear sizes fourteen to twenty. Don't you think more women would go, knowing that the others in the class were going to look just like them? (Are you listening, Jack La Lanne?)

I'll admit right off the bat that I've never been a big one for structured exercise. I abide by the philosophy of a

feisty seventy-eight-year-old woman I know. Jean is fit as
a fiddle and strong as a horse, and when you ask her about
exercise, she cocks one eyebrow and replies with some
disdain, "Exercise? Do you know how many people have
heart attacks while they're out *walking?*"

From time to time I've investigated the health clubs
that are a big rage now. But the exercise classes seem like
medieval torture chambers. To the deceptively upbeat
throb of music, the women in these classes cry out in
agony and scream with pain. Their faces are screwed up
in perpetual misery. Not my idea of a good time. And
frankly, it doesn't seem all that healthy to be so miserable.
Sometimes I wonder if the self-torture is really as much
about fitness as it is about letting their anger show. What
are they angry at?

The real function of exercise should be fitness, and you
might be surprised at how little exercise it really takes to
keep your cardiovascular system functioning healthily.
And I know that health is a concern for you because it's a
concern for every older person. We don't just want to live
longer—we want to live longer in the best possible shape.

Most authorities suggest that moderate exercise three
times a week can make a tremendous difference in the
way you look and feel. Walking is a great form of exercise.
So is playing golf. And a few minutes of stretching every
day will keep you flexible and help turn away the flab.
You don't have to pay thousands of dollars to join fancy
health clubs. Build your own exercise program. Enlist a
friend or two to join you and make it a social event.

I asked a number of doctors whom I trust, "What
would you tell women in their middle-to-older years who
are embarking on a modest exercise program for the first
time in their lives?" Here's the advice they gave me:

1. Check with your doctor before you begin. This is absolutely essential. It might seem that you're only going to be making minor changes in your routine, but it's still important to make sure you're up to it. (Incidentally, this is a good time for a checkup, anyway, especially if you're recently widowed. Stress can take a toll.)
2. Start slowly. You're not Jane Fonda. You never will be Jane Fonda. Just take things at your own pace. Walk around the block...don't run in the marathon! Overexercising is dangerous—it could be worse than no exercise at all. And be sure to always stretch out and warm up before you exercise to protect your muscles, ligaments and joints.
3. Set a schedule. Exercising regularly is more important than how long you exercise. The recommendation is three times a week.
4. Only exercise when you're feeling well. Even if you have a small cold or flu, don't exercise. Your system is already being challenged enough. Wait until you feel back to normal.
5. Don't get crazy. These are my words, not the doctors', but you see my point. It's easy to get caught up in the mania. Resist the temptation. Know yourself and your capabilities.

Size: Ample Not Sample

When it comes to weight, I contend that if God had wanted us to be skeletons, He wouldn't have put meat on our bones. I am offended by our culture's fanaticism about being thin and I refuse to buy it. In fact, there's a wonderful food store in New York called Zabar's and I just love going there. When I die, they've promised me I can be buried over the Scotch salmon.

I was in Zabar's the other day buying éclairs in the bakery and a woman, a perfect stranger, said to me, "You *eat* those?" I gave her a chilling look and replied, "Oh, no, of course not. I have a friend who eats them for me and she tells me how they taste."

Eating is a sensual pleasure, so why do we have to ruin it by sitting around the table discussing the relative nutritional benefits of every bite we put in our mouths? Why is it a sin to enjoy good food once in a while? And why should women go out with men who are so insecure that they think any woman with a little flesh on her is unattractive and undisciplined?

I had a date like that. This man took me to a lovely restaurant and we were seated at a beautiful table. As we were reading the menu, the waiter appeared. "May I offer you an appetizer?"

"No, thank you," my date replied, without so much as a glance in my direction. "Appetizers will fill us up too much. We won't have room for the main course."

So we ate our scanty main course. This was one of those restaurants that served nouvelle cuisine, which means they put a microscopic piece of meat in the center of your plate and surround it with beans and flowered radishes.

When we were finished, the waiter reappeared and asked, "May I show you a dessert menu?"

My date piped right up again. "No, nothing for us."

By now I was half starved and pretty annoyed, so I said brightly, "Nothing? Do you make a wonderful 'nothing' here?" While my date glared at me, I said, "I didn't say nothing. I'd love some dessert."

"You don't eat dessert, do you?" my date inquired with

the same degree of horror he might have brought to the question, "You don't eat small children, do you?"

I was furious! Why should I have to apologize for enjoying a little bit of life?

Some of the most beautiful women I've ever seen while traveling are the women in the rural and farm areas. These are big women. And they're gorgeous. Their husbands are big too. They're fat together and they're so happy. I have a feeling that they're also healthy.

But it's the curse of women who live in big cities to be caught up in the cosmopolitan obsession with weight. In a city like New York, where modeling is a big business, there's bound to be a mania about weight. As far as I'm concerned, a model is a hanger with a dress on it. Those are bodies? Come on!

I am the moderator for fashion shows in Florida that are sponsored by a department-store chain there. These are shows for women sizes fourteen to twenty. I call the shows "Ample Not Sample"—a reference to the fact that a sample size is usually an eight. Before I agree to moderate the shows, I warn the chain ahead of time, "You've got to let me be absolutely honest. And you've got to include two or three older women models or I won't do it. You've also got to have one or two models who are at least a size sixteen. I cannot, in all honesty, look at the women in the audience and say, 'You'll look wonderful in this,' when the model is a size eight."

Of course, they don't always follow through and sometimes they sneak an anorexic model in. I make it a comedy show. I say, "Yes, girls, and this dress will look marvelous hanging on a hanger in your closet."

Don't Kid Yourself

So, how is it possible to be fit and healthy and look our best without getting caught up in this madness? How do we learn to love ourselves the way we are? Never in my life have I been below a size fourteen. I'm five eight and I'm a big woman. But I always go out looking the best I can. I carry my clothes well and I love my life. I don't feel like a freak, and no person on earth is going to make me feel that way.

The key to the whole weight question, as far as I'm concerned, is to find the weight you're comfortable at and to stick with it. Don't measure yourself against anyone else's standards. The most damaging thing to both your health and your self-esteem is the desperate attempt to be someone you're not.

I saw a woman in a restaurant recently eating a piece of pizza. She was huge—her ankles were the size of an average thigh. She looked at me guiltily and said, "I'm going to stop eating this junk."

"Oh, really," I said, raising my eyebrows. "And may I ask how long you've been eating this junk?"

"About forty-five years," she admitted.

"My goodness! Do you mind if I ask you what this wonderful thing is that's going to free you? How are you planning to become emancipated from eating junk?"

"Oh," she said, "I'm having suction."

"You're having what?"

"They have a procedure now," she explained, "where they suck all the fat out."

"Ughh!" The thought made me shudder. "So what are you going to do about eating pizza and other junk once they suck all the fat out?"

She answered with great conviction. "Once I see myself thin, I won't want to eat anymore."

Such illusions!

My philosophy about weight loss is very simple. The first thing to do is look at yourself in the mirror and say, "I'm perfect just the way I am." And believe it. Only then can you decide that maybe you'd really like to lose a few pounds. Self-improvement is great if you go about it with a healthy attitude.

I have a friend who has tried every single diet that has ever been created. High protein, low fat, high carbohydrate, watermelon, fasting—you name it, she's given it a shot. Like most chronic dieters, she's lost hundreds of pounds in her lifetime . . . and gained them all back, too, as soon as boredom set in. Not too long ago, I ran into her at a party and she looked stunning. I had never seen her look so good.

"Finally you've found a successful diet!" I joked.

"No, I'm not dieting," she replied.

"Why, you look wonderful."

"I know," she said matter-of-factly. "One day I threw out all my diet books and decided to just live my life. It was such a relief. And I've lost weight, too, because I'm following what my stomach tells me, not what some book tells me."

Bravo for her. She'll never be pencil thin, but who cares? Beauty and radiance of this sort can only come from one place, and all the diets in the world won't make it happen.

Try a Little Plastic

I have never been able to understand why women feel so embarrassed to admit that they've had plastic surgery. Or why so many women think there's something wrong with having a face-lift. There is no reason in the world to feel funny about having plastic surgery. We change the color of our hair. We use makeup. What's so different about giving our faces a little lift when they need it? I know women who will diet to death, who will jog and exercise several hours a day, who will spend small fortunes on their hair and makeup. But when it comes to plastic surgery, they'll say, "I could never do that. It's not natural."

And there are women who say, "I'm proud of my wrinkles. They show that I've lived." Now, it's beyond me why anyone would cherish wrinkles and say, "Like a soldier wears his medals, I wear my wrinkles." Isn't that the most ridiculous thing you've ever heard? What's beautiful about wrinkles? They don't even look good on turtles and they were born wrinkled!

I'm proud of the results of my two face-lifts and I've always talked openly about them. I had my first face-lift in 1969, just after I left *Girl Talk* and was headed for California to star in a show under my own name. The second one came shortly after Harry died, when my ego was feeling particularly in need of a boost.

I was very naïve the first time I went through it. People just weren't talking about plastic surgery then—it was a deep dark secret. Although I found my doctor through "word of mouth," it is more accurate to say that I found him through "hint of mouth." Those who raved about him did so always because a good friend had used him. Never themselves!

When I went for my initial consultation, he suggested a "mini-lift." Just the eyes and neck. It didn't sound too drastic—a nip here, a tuck there—so I said, "Why not? What do I have to lose except the turkey that's been growing under my chin for the past few years?"

The next step in the process was a trip to a photographer who specialized in those charming "before" pictures. Now, this photographer bought his mirrors from the same company that supplied the Coney Island fun house. I was sure of it. When I looked in the mirror my face seemed so warped and flabby that I cried, "No doctor can help me!" Of course, the point of the mirrors is to make you appreciate even more fully the remarkable skill of the doctor who rescues you from a lifetime of deformity.

At this point in my life I felt that I was enough of a star that I should not use my stage name when I checked into the hospital. I signed in under my married name, Virginia Guttenberg. (I will say, however, that when I arrived at the hospital and wasn't immediately recognized, I was very insulted. Go figure that!) They took me to my room, where I noticed they had the same mirrors as there had been in the photographer's studio—this was so you wouldn't decide that you didn't look so bad after all and leave.

I was quite uninformed about the actual surgery. Before I entered the hospital I had my hair colored, shampooed and set as if I were going to the President's Ball. I was still thinking of the procedure as "a little nip and tuck" and I wanted to look my best. As I was sitting in my room, beautifully coiffed, the nurse walked in, carrying a king-sized bottle of Phisohex. We stared each other down for a moment before I asked politely, "What's that for?"

She heaved a big sigh. She knew she had a live one on her hands. "You have to shampoo your hair before we take you for tests."

I gave her a level gaze. "My dear, I'm sure that won't be necessary. I just had my hair professionally done two hours ago."

She faced me with eyes of steel. "Mrs. Guttenberg, you are having a face-lift. This is surgery, not the beauty parlor."

I laughed, relieved. "No, no, you've got the wrong chart. I'm not having a face-lift . . . just a mini-tuck."

"You are having a face-lift." She showed me the chart. "It's all here. Your doctor's name. Your name."

I was dumbstruck. "But," I sputtered, "I thought he was only doing the eyes and neck."

"That's a face-lift," she said wearily.

This exchange was very similar to the discussion I once had with my beauty operator when I went in for a trim and it cost fifty dollars. I said, "But I just asked for a trim." She replied, "The *minute* I take scissors in my hand and *touch* your hair, that's a cut."

So, now I knew the awful truth. I was having a face-lift. I stumbled meekly into the bathroom and washed my hair with the vile stuff. When I came out, the nurse had returned with a wheelchair. "Now we're going down to have a cardiogram and x-ray your chest and take blood."

"Wait a minute!" I was back on the warpath. "I'm just having my face done."

"It's surgery, my dear. Any time a knife is used—"

"A knife!"

She gave me a hopeless look. "Did you think we were going to use Silly Putty to rearrange your face? This is surgery."

By the time I had gone through a battery of tests, I

began to think about forgetting the whole thing. But I swallowed my terror and went through with it.

One of the hardest things about cosmetic surgery is facing how *terrible* you look immediately afterward. There's no possible way to prepare yourself for it. And no matter how many assurances you get that the swelling and bruising will go away, you never believe it. At my hospital, the nurse strictly warned me that I was not, under any circumstances, to look in a mirror. I was to pretend that all the mirrors had been taken from my room. Of course, my instant reaction was that even if I had to get up and hobble down the hall to the men's room to look in a mirror, I would do it. I had to see my face.

Silly, silly me. Although I had never seen the victim of a head-on collision, the face that stared back at me in the mirror had obviously been in an awful accident. I fell asleep that night contemplating a lifetime of deformity.

Naturally I ended up loving my new face and was proud to show off how good I looked. The procedure probably took ten years off my age and it gave me a rested, glowing look. I was thrilled.

Now, as I said before, in those days one did not speak of having plastic surgery. It was the great taboo. But I broke the silence barrier on the *Merv Griffin Show.*

When I walked out, Merv rose to his feet and gushed, "Virginia, you look simply wonderful."

"I should," I replied without hesitation. "I just had my face done."

There was a moment of dead silence while Merv digested this incredible announcement. Then he sprang to life. "You *what!*" He was looking at me as though I had openly admitted to the commission of a murder. "What are you talking about, Virginia?" This kind of revelation is what talk-show hosts live for. I could tell this was a major high point of Merv's life. "I can't believe you're saying this. Here you are, sitting in front of twenty-five million people—"

"Is that your rating, Merv?" I interrupted. "That's wonderful."

"—and you're saying that you just had a face-lift?"

Thinking, "The man is deaf," I repeated very slowly, "Yes-I-am-telling-people-that-I-just-had-a-face-lift."

Merv was determined to milk this announcement for all it was worth. "How can you admit it?"

"I'll tell you the truth, Merv. If a few of you men would look in the mirror, you'd get the name of my doctor."

The audience howled at this, but Merv was taken aback. "You're not telling me that I should have a face-lift?"

Winking at the audience, I said fervently, "Oh, no, not *you*, Merv. You're God and God never ages. Besides, I'm a guest on your show. You're paying me. If you had wrinkles down to your knees I wouldn't tell you. But I'm not ashamed to admit that I had my face done. I did it because I want to be a performer for many years to come, and if I don't televise well, I'm in trouble. After all, people diet and they do other things. Let's just say I dieted. I lost half my face."

That was my first face-lift. The second time around, the procedure went more smoothly. I was prepared for it. And that time I really needed it. My face was flabby and I was tired and drawn-looking from enduring Harry's long illness and death. I was also at an age when I thought I could kiss good looks good-bye. After all, I was on my third set of teeth. And the world seemed to open up to me in a new way after my plastic surgery.

Transforming the way you look can give you that extra boost of self-confidence you need to get back out into the world. But I caution you to be realistic about what to expect from plastic surgery. Are you expecting a hidden genie to emerge and change you completely? Do you think that your long-dormant beauty will suddenly come rushing to the surface? That you will suddenly be more witty, more charming, a more dazzling companion? These changes come from the inside! Can you wipe away your bereavement by having a face-lift? No. Can having a face-lift make you feel less pain? No. Can a face-lift give you a better chance to go back into the world and meet people and start over again? Yes.

But I urge you to get plenty of consultation before you take the plunge. Check out the doctors. Ask around. Get several opinions. And don't listen to your friends! Nobody's going to have the real answer but you. And if the doctor is a good one, plastic surgery can be much simpler than you expect. Here are a few guidelines I've put together from my experience in choosing a plastic surgeon:

1. Go to at least two doctors, maybe three, before making your decision. Make sure you check the professional credentials and board certification of each doctor. Ask your doctor the most specific details of the effects of the surgery. Know, for example, that an eye-lift doesn't erase wrinkles—it just eliminates the bags under your eyes.
2. Check the doctor's hospital affiliation. Some hospitals are better than others and you want your stay to be as comfortable as possible.
3. Don't be afraid to talk to the people in the doctor's waiting room to get a sense of how they feel about him and how he treats his patients.
4. Ask if you can talk to any of his former patients. This might not be possible, since people value their

privacy, but if the opportunity is there, jump at it. (Chances are, you've already seen the results of his work in the friends who recommended him to you in the first place.)

5. Make sure the doctor is open and thorough in discussing the procedure and the risks. Yes, there are always risks in surgery, and don't let anyone tell you differently. Be prepared. Do as much reading as possible about the various procedures available.

6. It's a bad sign if you don't like your doctor or if you don't feel comfortable with him. You're embarking on a very intimate project together. It's important that you trust him and feel good about your rapport.

A face-lift won't change your personality. All plastic surgery does is improve the look of the package. What's inside is up to you.

Only Skin Deep

Are you concerned that your physical beauty is too vain a pursuit? They say that beauty is only skin deep—but since none of my friends have x-ray vision, skin deep is good enough for me! I wasn't blessed with perfect looks, but I take great pride and delight in keeping myself looking the very best I can. I put on makeup to greet delivery men! It's a point of pride. Excellent grooming can be achieved simply and inexpensively. I haven't used soap on my face since I was sixteen, but I don't use expensive creams either. I use good old reliable Ponds. It has always worked for me, so there's been no reason for me to go out and buy lavish skin products.

The most important beauty secret I've learned is this:

If you have dark rings under your eyes, always use a light concealing cream under your foundation. Dark circles can pull your face down and add at least ten years to your age.

Another trick that will help you look younger is to color the hair that frames your face a slightly lighter shade than the rest. It will achieve a halo effect that's lovely. Speaking of hair color, I don't know a woman alive over a certain age who doesn't need it. It can be expensive to have your hair colored professionally, but I'd say that more than a third of my friends color their own hair and get terrific results at home, using the one-step shampooing processes that are available for under ten dollars.

Always use a perfume that best reflects your personality. Make it your trademark! I stay away from heavy scents and am always careful about how much I apply. Too much perfume is nauseating! Our scent is a very sensual and powerful element of our presentation to the outside world. So, take care that your perfume sends just the right signals.

Let's face it. There are a million tricks that will improve your looks. And I'm happy to share what I know. But you are finally the architect of your own beauty, both the kind that comes from within and the kind that shines on the outside. Take pride in yourself and love the person that looks back at you in the mirror. That's the first step. Then have fun discovering with paint and polish just how glamorous and beautiful you really can be!

❖ 6 ❖

Merry Widows in the World

The first couple of times I called Helen, I got her answering machine with the message, "Hello, this is Helen. I can't come to the phone right now..."

I knew she was there. "Helen!" I screamed at the machine. "Pick up the phone. Stop hiding from me." No answer, just the dead silence of an empty line.

Answering machines are a great invention, but they also make it easier for people to hide. And I knew Helen was hiding. Her husband, Bill, had passed away six months earlier. During the mourning period Helen had been a rock. She was a courtly woman with a flair for entertaining and making people feel comfortable. Even grief couldn't mask her special glow as she accepted the condolences of her friends. But when it was all over,

Helen simply dropped out of sight. I left her alone for a while—I could remember my own exhaustion after Harry had died. But now, I figured, it was about time Helen got on with her life. If only I could reach her.

Over several weeks I left increasingly threatening messages on her machine. Finally, one day I said, "Helen, if you don't return this call within twenty-four hours I'm going to call the police."

She picked up the phone. "I give up," she said wearily.

I sighed with relief. "It's about time . . . how are you, darling?"

Her voice was low and strangely devoid of expression. "I'm okay, I guess. A little tired."

"Yes," I agreed. "Grief can really knock the wind out of your sails . . . but, Helen, it's been six months now. I think you'd feel better if you got out a little."

"I don't know, Virginia."

"Well, I *do* know. Are you free for lunch tomorrow?"

We met for lunch at an elegant and charming little French restaurant. I saw immediately that Helen did not look very well. In six months she had aged ten years. Something had to be done.

As she was picking at her endive, I suddenly said, "Maybe you should just go ahead and follow Bill. It's obvious that you can't live without him."

"What?" She jerked her head up. "What on earth do you mean?"

"Helen," I said gently, "you know I love you. And I'm concerned. Look at you. You're death warmed over."

Tears bubbled to the surface of her eyes. "I'm trying, but I just can't seem to get any energy up."

"I understand how you feel. I went through exactly the same thing when Harry died. You know, there are stages of grief—it takes time to get through them. But I also think that the longer you hide yourself from the world, the harder it will be to get back." I patted her arm. "Helen, your friends miss you. It's time you put Bill to rest."

She nodded. "I know you're right, but what can I do?"

"What can you do? *You,* the most talented hostess in New York? Helen, you've completely lost your perspective, not to mention your nerve. Here's what I think you should do. I think you should have a dinner party. Just a small one for a few of your closest friends."

"Do you think they'd come?"

I shook my head in exasperation. "Of course they would. Helen, have you had a stroke? You don't seem to be playing with a full deck here."

Through much cajoling, I finally convinced Helen to have a dinner for eight people—three couples, a widower who was a friend of her family, and me. Since she had temporarily lost her touch, I held her hand through all the preparations. She begged me to come early and I obliged.

The table was already set when I walked in and everything looked perfect. I had a feeling this would be a happy evening.

When I saw Helen, I gasped. "You look wonderful!" I cried. "You actually have color in your cheeks." It was true. Helen looked better than she had in months. Her face was flushed with excitement.

"I'm glad you talked me into this," she told me. "Even if I am a little nervous."

"Don't be silly. These are just friends. They're not going to bite."

As the guests arrived, each one of them pulled Helen into a tight embrace. Everyone had really missed her. We sat around talking and laughing and sipping cocktails.

One man had us collapsed in giggles with his funny stories about Bill. Even Helen was laughing. I kept thinking, "This is perfect, just perfect."

Suddenly I noticed that Helen wasn't in the room. "Uh oh," I thought, and went to look for her.

I found her sitting at the vanity table in her bedroom, dabbing tears from her eyes. I put my arm around her. "Oh, Helen," I said, "I know it's hard, but—"

She held up a hand to stop me. "No, no, you've got it all wrong. I'm fine, really. I was just so overcome with happiness to have such wonderful friends...oh, Virginia, thank you for this!"

Widowhood brings on a kind of temporary insanity. We forget for a while who we are. Our heads get cluttered with bizarre thoughts like

- "Nobody is going to want to be with me...my friends only liked me because of him."
- "I'll just be a fifth wheel."
- "The fun years are over."
- "Maybe I should just join a convent."

One of the best things about marriage is that you have a companion who is there, always there. Your place in the world is strengthened by your attachment. Your calendar is secured. When you suddenly find yourself alone, your mind fills with a thousand nagging fears. The thought of a Christmas Day without him brings tears to your eyes. When Valentine's Day approaches, the reminder that there will be no roses this year sends you into despair. During the month when you always shared a vacation trip, the realization that there will never be another one turns the sunny days bleak. You are struck with the reality that you no longer have an automatic date every Saturday night. You feel less confident about picking up the phone and calling your married friends. Surely they're too busy for you.

You feel alone.

In the wonderful book *How to Survive the Loss of a Love*, there is a poem by Peter McWilliams that goes:

> I found
> in you
> a home.
> Your departure
> left me a
> Shelterless Victim
> of a
> Major Disaster.
> I called the
> Red Cross
> but they
> refused to
> send over
> a nurse.

If that's the way you feel, join the club. It may console you to know that every widow feels this way. But there comes a time when your grief isn't enough to sustain you and it's time to get moving.

Your lifelong friends are not going to automatically desert you once you're widowed. To the contrary, many of them will rally round. But you also have to make the effort to get out on your own and build a new circle of friends. Why is this necessary? Because you are no longer the same woman you were before. Your lifestyle has changed.

One word of advice, though. Don't be too hard on your

friends and neighbors if they seem a little uncertain at first about approaching you. It's a shame that we can't be more open about the realities of death. After all, it's a prospect we most certainly all face. But most people are uncomfortable about it. Your friends may care very deeply for you, but they're probably confused about how to approach you. "Should I try to cheer her up and make her laugh?" "Should I be solemn and tearful?" "Does she really want to be invited out now?" Sometimes you'll have to make the first move, *not* because your friends don't care, but because they're trying to be compassionate.

Time for Fun

A group of women I know have met for lunch every Tuesday for the past five years. Rain or shine. Ups or downs. It's rare for any of them to miss the occasion. I asked one of them why the lunches were so special and she laughed. "It's fun," she said simply. I bet it is, too. It's such a simple thing, having lunch with friends. Gossiping and chatting and telling jokes. But what therapy that can be for a woman living alone! The woman added that "sometimes in the middle of these lunches I completely forget what it feels like to be sad or lonely. It's just such a satisfying way to spend an afternoon."

Another woman I know nursed her husband through a serious illness that lasted nearly two years. In the end, he carried around a portable oxygen tank, and she had to be by his side every minute. At night she was always half awake, with one ear cocked to hear the sound of his breathing.

"I didn't know how exhausted I was until after he died," she reflected. "Then, suddenly, everything caved

in. One day I realized with a shock that I hadn't had *any*
fun for more than two years!"

The myth of the "merry widow" makes us all smile
because it's such an outrageous notion. We're not exactly
in a position to kick up our heels, are we? Maybe not
quite. But there's no time or age limit on fun. And now's
your chance to do things you've never done.

"Like what?" you may ask. Perhaps your mind is a
blank. Start by promising yourself that you won't rule out
any possibility (except, maybe, mountain climbing if
you're an older woman). Here are a few ideas to get you
started:

1. Start a lunch club like the one I spoke about. It's
   easy enough to do. Just start calling your friends.
   You can probably think of a number of other women
   who are alone. If your budget is tight, make it a
   deli lunch at home and have everyone chip in ten
   dollars. It may become the most important item on
   your monthly budget.
2. Establish a "dining-out night" once a week or once
   every two weeks. Make it less often if money is
   short, but make it special. Reserve your "table for
   one" at a restaurant you love (maybe even one that
   you and your husband enjoyed together). You might
   want to invite a different friend or relative to join
   you each week. They will definitely learn to think
   of it as "an occasion."
3. Take up a sport. When my friend Judy told me she
   was taking golf lessons, I nearly split my sides
   laughing. "You?" I cried. "You're kidding. The most
   exercise I've ever seen you get is carrying your
   shopping bag from Saks to the taxi. What's this
   sudden interest in sports?"

"A friend of mine belongs to a club with her husband," she explained. "And they invited me along once and I enjoyed myself. It felt so good to be outdoors and it's actually fun. Besides," she added with a devilish grin, "you wouldn't believe all the men that hang around golf courses."

If you've never been particularly active, take it slow and know your limits. There are a number of sports that are perfectly safe for older women— golfing, swimming, walking, and even tennis.

There are also activities that might not be officially called "sports," but which involve plenty of sport. I know a woman who takes a bus to Atlantic City every Wednesday to play the slot machines. There are all kinds of specials for senior citizens. Her bus trip is free and she's given fifteen dollars in chips. In addition, she budgets another twenty dollars and has the time of her life.

4. Join a club. There is probably a club in existence for every known interest. If you've never considered yourself a "joiner" before, you may have no idea where to start. The best place to start is in your own mind. What do you enjoy? What are your interests? Clubs are simply groups of people who share a common interest. A woman I know in New York set up a cooking club with six other people. Each week they gather at a different member's house and the host cooks a fabulous creation. It's more social than anything, although the talk tends to focus around the meal. It sounds like a lot of fun to me. Another woman, a poet, began advertising that she was going to host poetry readings in her home every Sunday evening. She invited aspiring poets to come and read to the group. She says that

the thing she most enjoys is the "odd collection" of people she meets, young and old alike.

5. Establish a new routine. Are you "stuck in your ways"? Maybe this isn't something you've really noticed, but think for a minute: Do you always go to the grocery store at exactly the same hour of the day? Do you always attend the same service at your church or synagogue? Is your hair appointment always on Thursday afternoon? Do you take your walk every day at two o'clock?

What would happen if you varied your routine? I think it would change the flavor of your life more than you might imagine and give you the opportunity to meet new people.

6. Enlist a friend and plan a vacation. Get away from your own acre and see a little of the world. You owe it to yourself. I'm a huge fan of cruises. They're ideal places to meet people, because when you're at sea for a long period of time, you can't help but develop a special closeness to the other people on the ship. And I don't necessarily mean *men*. In fact, about the only way you're going to meet an available man is if you throw his wife overboard. But you can meet true friends. And if what you really want is to meet a man, sometimes the best way to accomplish that is to expand your circle of friends.

Time to Throw a Party

In her book *Formerly Married*, Marilyn Jensen relates the story of a woman whose husband died. She went through the same process of grief that we're all so familiar with. But then, as she tells it, "It was Christmastime when I think I really turned the corner. Alan had been dead for only three months and Christmas had been a very important time for us. My daughter came home and we decided to have a party—an open house for close friends, people who had been supportive to us. I heard later that some people thought it strange that we should be having a party, but I know now it was the best thing I could have done for myself. It made me feel and experience the continuity of life—to be able to entertain friends. And I was letting them know that I was opening up my life to them. Instead of deciding to be alone or waiting to be invited, I was inviting them into *my* home and *my* life."

Isn't that a beautiful sentiment? As my friend Helen discovered, inviting friends into your home can open up the floodgates of love and support that you're seeking.

I love to entertain. There's no glow that is as warm as the one you feel when you're in your home surrounded by your friends.

Of course, I realize that in addition to your insecurity you might also be concerned about more practical matters, such as the cost or what to serve or whether to have the party catered. When your husband was there, it seemed a lot easier to entertain because you handled it like a team. Now you have to figure out how to juggle everything by yourself.

The best way to go about it is to ask a good friend to help you plan the party and make preparations. Get some help, especially the first time you try it.

Just remember that inviting people into your home is the greatest compliment you can pay them, so don't be shy about it. And nobody is going to care if you entertain inexpensively. I rarely have formal dinners anymore because it seems that all my friends want to be more casual these days. The important thing is to get people together, not to impress them with your elaborate style of entertaining.

Don't limit your ideas about entertaining to dinners— how dull! There are so many different ways to bring people together. I love sports, and during the football season I'll have people over to watch the games and all I'll serve is deli sandwiches. Other easy ways of entertaining include having brunches, informal dinners and potluck picnics.

SUNDAY BRUNCH

Around New York, Sunday brunch has become the "in" thing. It's usually held between one o'clock and four o'clock, when people are most relaxed. One of the nice things about brunch is that it can be either extremely casual or very elegant. When I have brunch, I usually invite five or six people and serve a French toast invention of mine that is so spectacular that I'm sure it will be served on the last day of the world.

Heavenly French Toast

SERVES SIX PEOPLE.
1 loaf challah bread
1 dozen eggs
1 cup heavy cream
¼ cup milk
1 teaspoon vanilla
Salt
Butter

PREPARATION:
Cut the challah bread into thick slices (a minimum of 2½ inches thick). Lay them flat in a pan that has been prepared with oil or Pam. Beat the eggs hard, then add the cream, milk, vanilla and a pinch of salt. Pour the mixture over the bread and refrigerate overnight, basting occasionally.

COOKING:
Melt butter in a saucepan over very low heat. Cook each piece in the butter (not more than 3 minutes), turning as each side browns.

SERVING:
Serve with hot maple syrup and butter. Very crisp bacon or ham is an excellent accompaniment to this dish.

INFORMAL DINNER
Many of us grew up with the notion that when you invite friends to dinner, it has to be a big deal—a platter of meat, a variety of vegetables, and so forth. But all that formality is not necessary. I frequently set up buffets, and I think my friends enjoy sitting around the living room balancing plates on their laps. On these occasions I often serve a vegetarian goulash that is delicious and a snap to prepare. I serve this dish with baked potatoes, sour cream and chives and a loaf of hot bread with garlic butter.

Vegetarian Goulash

Red, green and yellow peppers
Chopped onion

Chopped fresh mushrooms
Chopped black olives
Butter or margarine
Salt

PREPARATION:
Slice the peppers very thin and sauté in butter, adding chopped onions, olives, mushrooms and a hearty dash of salt. That's all there is to it!

POTLUCK PICNIC
If you have a nice yard, it's fun to have a potluck picnic during the summer months. You prepare the meat part of the meal (hamburgers, hot dogs, barbecued chicken, etc.) and supply the condiments and drinks. Your guests bring salads, breads, and desserts.

Let me say a word here about asking your guests to share the burden of your entertaining. I used to believe that it was really tacky to invite people to a meal and then turn around and ask them to bring their own food. If anyone asked, "Can I bring something?" my standard answer would be a firm no. I thought I was doing them a favor, until a friend pointed out just the opposite. "Virginia, you've got it completely backward," he told me. "It makes people feel good to share. You're taking that away from them." Good advice!

PARTY IDEAS
A party can be built around anything. It's more fun if you use your imagination. In this day and age, parties have lost a lot of the sparkle I remember them having in my youth. A woman I know who is seventy-nine had a party recently and there were a lot of young people there

because she invited her grandchildren and their friends, too. Midway through the evening she announced that they were going to play party games. The young people looked at her as if she had completely lost her marbles. But, of course, everyone had a rollicking time.

Themes for parties are endless: Have a party on Academy Awards night; host a holiday party; invite your contemporaries to a nostalgia party; if you have a VCR, rent movies and serve popcorn and beer. Use your imagination. I know a woman here in the city who had a party in February when the New York winter was at its cruelest. It was a "beach party." She had everyone come in beach clothes and she spread out towels, passed out sunglasses and served hot dogs, potato salad and beer. Wisely, she included on the invitation: "No sand, please."

◈ 7 ◈

Get in Gear

Before you can really begin living anew, you will need to clear the air with yourself. I'd like to ask you a few questions as a way of oiling up the thought process. Be completely honest. Nobody is going to see your answers but you, and no purpose is ever served by fibbing to yourself. Just answer yes or no.

1. Do you believe that it's impossible to begin a career when you are over a certain age? ____
2. When asked to describe your talents, do you have trouble thinking of anything to say? ____
3. Are you shy when you're in groups? ____
4. Are you frequently "put down" by people close to

you for voicing your opinions—or for the tasks you accomplish? _____

5. When you describe yourself, do you use the term "old"? _____
6. Do you spend a lot of time daydreaming about the past, going through old photo albums, etc.? _____
7. Do you harbor a belief that your education is inadequate or that you're not very smart? _____
8. Do you feel unhappy if you don't talk with your children every day? _____
9. When your husband was alive, did you envy him because he seemed to have more freedom than you, or because he seemed to accomplish more? _____
10. When you look at the next five years, do you draw a blank about what you'll be doing? _____
11. Even if you have professional skills, do you have serious doubts that you could get hired because of your age? _____
12. Do you think in terms of "retirement," not in terms of "reentry"? _____

If you answered yes to any of these questions, you have a problem with self-esteem that is very common among older women. Yet, I suspect that deep down inside, you'd really like to find something fulfilling to do—a grand last hurrah. You've probably observed many older women who are doing important things, but you think they're the exception rather than the rule. ("I think it's wonderful that Lillian Carter joined the Peace Corps at her age...she must have incredible genes.")

Especially if you've never had a career or been actively involved in volunteer work, you may have *no idea* what you can do, what you're good at, what you would enjoy.

How do you find that out? You have to look inside because nobody's going to tell you.

A friend of mine who is sixty-two and who never went to college called me one day to share some news. Ruth had been a devoted wife and she had loved raising her six children. It fulfilled her and made her happy. But now, with her husband gone and the kids grown, she was casting about for something new to do. "This will sound silly to you," she told me shyly, "but I've signed up for a writing course at the community college."

"That's wonderful—why on earth would I think it's silly?"

"I was never a very good student. I don't have ambitions to be a great writer. It's just something I've always wanted to do."

"Maybe you'll be a great writer and maybe you won't," I said. "Just jump in with both feet. It's wonderful that you're able to pursue a lifelong interest."

It was brave of Ruth to go back to school, but she still didn't believe in herself. It took glowing praise from her teacher on a short story she had written to make her feel the tiniest bit confident. "He liked it!" she said in shock. I just smiled.

To find your niche in the world you have to conduct an honest self-examination. Here are a few more questions to ask yourself:

1. As a child, what activities interested you most?
2. What careers and community involvements did members of your family have?
3. What were your dreams when you were eighteen?
4. If you made motherhood a career, what were the things you enjoyed most about being a mother? (Be as specific as possible.)

5. How would you describe your personality?
6. Describe the happiest time in your life. What were you doing at the time?
7. Have you ever had an interest in something that you didn't pursue because you were too busy or lacked proper credentials?
8. For the last twenty years, list one key accomplishment for each year. (This will take some time. Maybe family and friends can refresh your memory about what happened each year.) The accomplishment can be *anything*.
9. Do you belong to a church or synagogue? If so, list the activities that are available there.
10. Finish this sentence: "If I wasn't too old, I'd . . ."

Reflecting in this way will begin to illuminate your abilities and interests. And let me stress one thing: Every person in the world is talented at something. Talent isn't just an "above the norm" ability. It's the essence of who you are. You may be a talented mother. Or talented at consoling friends in need. Or a talented cook. Or talented at making people laugh. All of these are qualities that can be applied, if you wish, in a practical way.

In his book *Success Over Sixty*, Albert Myers relates this story: "'A little bingo, dinner with friends and lots of doing nothing,' is the way Ruth Bennett described her existence at seventy-eight. That was before she unintentionally stole the show at a roast honoring her son Alex, a disc jockey on San Francisco's hard-rock station, KMEL, 106.1 FM. The next day, a station executive asked her if she would be interested in hosting her own rock 'n' roll show. At first she laughed the offer off, but a few days later she changed her mind. Since then, Ruth, the widow of a violinist, has delighted her radio fans every Sunday night by spinning hit singles . . ."

The world is full of oldies making it. And if you look closely at these people, you'll see that the two main elements of their success are confidence in themselves and a sheer love of life.

For years a woman I know grew her own herbs in a little greenhouse in her backyard. We were all the beneficiaries of her wonderful skill. I can still remember the lovely scent of fresh mint wafting from my kitchen counter. After her husband died she continued her hobby. And one day a man she knew who owned a specialty food store approached her. "I wonder if you'd be interested in having a small display of your herbs in my store," he proposed.

"You mean for sale?" she asked, surprised.

"Of course," he said, laughing. "I'd love to sell fresh herbs and I think my customers would jump at the chance to buy them."

"I knew nothing about business," she related to me later. "I mean, how much do you charge for something that you've been giving away for twenty years? At first I'm sure I underpriced them. And when they started selling fast, I almost panicked. I was afraid I'd never be able to keep up with it. Finally I hired my granddaughter, who is sixteen, to help me. We had a marvelous time working together. It was her idea to set up gift packs for the holidays and they sold out the first week.

"You know," she told me, "for the first time in my life I really feel like I'm accomplishing something on my own. I'm even considering joining a local businesswomen's group. What do you think of that?"

Sometimes the solution to your dilemma— "What do I

do?"—is right under your nose, but you're too close to recognize it.

One Door Closes, Another Opens

I wasn't exactly a budding youth when I started my career in television. Furthermore, I had no formal training whatsoever for this pursuit. My career evolved from very pedestrian beginnings: the hosting duties I performed at charity luncheons when I was a housewife in Great Neck, New York.

Shortly before I began my television career I was thinking my life was over. I had just had cancer surgery and the doctors told me frankly that they didn't expect me to live for long. Harry was very ill at the time. I looked around and saw my life crumbling before my eyes. Although I had always been strong in times of crisis, this was just too much to bear. I could find no hope at all for a future.

At the time, I was doing small jobs, and one day I was serving as the mistress of ceremonies for a beauty pageant being run by my brother-in-law. At lunchtime we took a break and went to a place on Fifty-fifth Street in New York called Billy Reed's Little Club. The dollar-seventy-five luncheon special included a chicken sandwich, coconut cake... and a psychic reading. The reader's name was Joanne Case, and when my turn came, she looked me squarely in the eye and said, "I'm sitting in front of one of the most important women in America."

I craned my neck around to take a look, thinking perhaps Eleanor Roosevelt had just walked into the restaurant. Joanne Case continued to look at me and I felt suddenly very nervous.

"You don't mean me?" I said, laughing.

"I certainly do mean you," she replied with calm conviction.

Now I really laughed. Here I was on my last legs from cancer, with no talent that I could identify, being told by a lunch-counter psychic that I was destined to become famous.

"Look," I told her, "I can't sing or dance. Today I'm hosting a beauty pageant and it's practically the first thing I've ever done. What are you talking about?"

"You're going to be famous," she insisted. "Tell me, what is your name?"

"Virginia Guttenberg."

"No, no." She shook her head. "That's all wrong. You are going to change your name to Virginia Graham and you are going to be one of the most successful women in America. Believe me."

I paid my dollar-seventy-five and went back to the beauty show, amused by the incident, but hardly taking it seriously.

The very next day I received a telephone call from the producer of a new television show called *Food for Thought*.

"My wife saw you speak at a fund-raiser for Cerebral Palsy," he told me, "and she's been hounding me to get you as a host for this show. Since my wife has never expressed admiration for another woman in her life, I figure that this is something I have to see. Can you come in?"

Before I knew it, I was hosting my first television show. Just like that. And, in deference to Joanne Case, I immediately changed my name to Virginia Graham.

Afterward, when I became successful, I tried to find Joanne Case, but Billy Reed had sold his restaurant and nobody knew where she was. But I often thought of her over the years, and felt that the dollar-seventy-five lunch was somehow a turning point in my life.

Many years later when I was doing *Girl Talk,* Nora Ephron, the writer, called me for an interview. In the course of our conversation she suddenly asked, "Do you believe in spiritualism?"

I shrugged. "Not really. I believe we make our own destiny. Although I will tell you a funny story." Nora listened quietly as I related the Joanne Case episode that heralded the launch of my career. "Wouldn't it be wonderful to see her and tell her all the things that have happened to me since that day?" I mused.

Nora grinned. "She's waiting for your call."

"What?"

"Joanne Case is my reader," she explained. "When I told her I was interviewing you, she told me to please give you her love and tell you that you may not remember her, but you met many years ago."

"Not remember her! I've been looking for her all these years."

I called and arranged with Joanne's secretary to pay her a visit. She was very frail when I saw her, but she still had a little sparkle of wisdom in her eyes. She took my hand and held it tightly. "I've followed your career every step of the way," she said. "I just knew when I met you that you were destined to be a great woman."

I was terribly moved, and the words spilled out of me in a rush. "Why didn't you get in touch with me? I would have loved to speak with you, but I could never find you. I wanted to tell you how outlandish your predictions seemed to me that day and how I never imagined that meeting you would become one of the high points of my life."

She said, "I'm very gratified that things have turned out the way they have for you."

"Oh, yes, it's been wonderful. But I must tell you, the day I spoke with you I was in such despair. My husband was ill, I thought my own life was over, but your words gave me such courage. Even if there had been no truth in your predictions, you inspired me and motivated me to rise out of my despair."

She gave me a long thoughtful look, then said, "I'm glad I could offer a word of encouragement. But never lose sight of the fact that it was your own determination, your own will to live and succeed, that made the difference in your life."

There is so much transition in all of our lives. When Harry died I was very successful and independent, and yet I was accosted by the fear that my life might really be over. But I took myself to task and I said, "Look, Virginia, Harry's gone. Are you going to jump into the grave with him? Are you going to subject yourself to a life sentence of solitary confinement and failure just because he's no longer in your life?"

And once again I managed to tap the wellsprings of strength inside me. I knew I would be okay, that I would be embarking on a new adventure. I saw this as an opportunity to go out into the world and try new things.

An obstetrician friend of mine once remarked to me, joking, that the reason babies cry when they're born is that they know they're going to be on their own and never again have the protection and safety of the womb. "It's like they're hollering, 'Hey! Wait a minute! What are you doing... put me back!'" It's a funny image, but it holds a kernel of truth.

Maybe you're screaming now, "Put me back!" And the more you focus on what you've lost, the less prepared you are to recognize what you're gaining.

A *Million Options*

Would you just laugh if I told you that you have literally a million options for things you can do? I mean *work* things, money-making pursuits. If you answered the questions I posed earlier in this chapter about your abilities and interests, you're ready to start looking at some practical ideas.

To help you along, let's look at several "types" of women—their personalities, backgrounds, etc.—and see if we can generate lists of career possibilities that might be available to them. This is a game, in a way—it's spinning dreams. But I've found that you first need dreams before you can undertake a serious endeavor.

PROFILE ONE: Nell is a widow in her sixties who never worked. She and her husband made lots of friends over the years, but basically Nell was a homebody. She was just too busy with her home and family to get too involved in community or church affairs, except very occasionally. If asked to describe Nell, her friends might note the following things:

- A private person, but very kind
- Hates crowds and very large groups of people
- Understanding of people in trouble
- An excellent seamstress
- Loves her home and takes good care of it
- Soft-spoken
- A wonderful cook
- Loves children and is very patient with them

• • •

Now, considering all these things about Nell, what are some of the things she might pursue?

1. Giving sewing lessons at home
2. Holding cooking classes for high-school girls
3. Selling her handiwork at boutiques
4. Providing catered goodies for small parties
5. Baby-sitting
6. Consulting on interior design
7. Working part time for a suicide prevention service
8. Baking pastries for sale in pastry stores

PROFILE TWO: Ann is a widow in her early seventies who is in good health, but has trouble getting around because of a poor hip. When she was younger she worked at several jobs, such as saleswoman in a department store and assistant in the editorial department of a publishing company. Her friends might describe her this way:

• Witty and sociable
• Intelligent, loves to read
• Informed on current events
• Loves to talk
• Enjoys meeting different kinds of people
• A very poetic writer
• A good typist
• A compassionate listener

With her personality and skills, Ann could pursue the following jobs:

1. Telephone solicitor or salesperson
2. Manuscript typist

3. Writer for greeting-card companies
4. Clipping-service employee
5. Free-lance public relations person
6. Reader for a publishing company
7. Telephone answering service employee
8. Tutor

PROFILE THREE: Marjory is a widow in her late fifties who has always been on the go. Although she's never worked at a paying job, she's been very involved in local charities all her life, among them, the hospital auxiliary and the Red Cross. She has also worked for political candidates, doing phone work and coordinating itineraries. Her friends might describe her this way:

- Full of energy
- Smart and well organized
- Interested in people
- A talented fund-raiser
- Attractive, looks younger than her age
- Warm and instantly likable
- Passionate about the things she cares about

So, what would be some career opportunities Marjory might consider?

1. Travel agent
2. Money-raiser for local colleges or institutions
3. Service matchmaker (you need something, she finds it)
4. Tour guide
5. Personal shopper
6. Party and social-event planner

PROFILE FOUR: In her early sixties, Barbara is an out-doorswoman. When her husband was alive they used to go on frequent camping trips and played golf almost every weekend during good weather. She still loves to be out-doors, although she hasn't been camping since he died. She spends many hours each week tending her luscious garden. Barbara's friends describe her this way:

- A talented "green thumb" in the garden
- Bursting with health, in good physical condition
- Dynamite on the golf course
- Patient and industrious
- Sociable and frank in conversation
- Loves animals

What might Barbara do to utilize her skills and special qualities?

1. Supply flowers to local florists
2. Begin a free-lance floral gift business
3. Start a newsletter for campers
4. Become a private golf instructor
5. Become a gardener or landscaper
6. Work for a pet-care service
7. Be a summer-camp administrator

Are you beginning to get the knack of this game? Okay, it's your turn. Do the same exercise for yourself. Ask your friends to tell you what they think are your most market-able qualities. And think about turning them into profit-able, sociable enterprises!

If you think some of these ideas are farfetched, listen to this story. Sarah, a woman in her mid-sixties, when faced with life alone, decided to do something she'd always wanted to do. Her children were horrified. Her friends were speechless. But she went ahead. Today, Sarah is a forest ranger in the hillside surrounding Lake Tahoe. She reports that life has never been so rich.

Back to School

I'm sure you've heard it said before that we never stop learning until the day we die. Yet most people believe there is a time limit on formal education. "School is for the young." Nonsense. Fortunately, many local community colleges have established programs for older people. These programs include *real job training*—they're not just "nice ways for seniors to spend their days."

A friend of mine noted wistfully one day that she was sorry she had never pursued her real estate license. "I started studying many years ago, but then Dick had his heart attack, so I stopped. It's too bad. I'd love to be doing that now."

"Are you planning to leave this earth in the near future?" I asked impatiently.

"No, I hope not."

"So, go back and finish your studies, you idiot," I advised her.

She did. And contrary to her fears, nobody thought it was the least bit peculiar that a sixty-five-year-old woman was taking the class. If anything, they admired her, and fondly called her "Mom."

Just look at some of the things you can learn now that can launch you in a career:

• • •

1. Take knitting and crochet classes. Or pottery lessons. The products of your work can be sold at gift shops and boutiques.
2. Learn computer programming. It's not as scary as you might imagine.
3. Take courses in restaurant management or bartending. (You're probably already an expert in food shopping and preparation.)
4. Learn to be a travel agent.
5. Become a practical nurse. It takes only about two years to train.

But above all, don't let your learning capacities atrophy while you sit around thinking you're too old.

Give Life's Gift

Janet was miserable when I spoke to her several months after her husband's death. "I'm afraid I'll never have anyone special in my life again," she confided. "I feel so alone."

I kidded her a little. "How can you feel alone in New York City, where you can't walk down the street without bashing elbows with hundreds of people?"

"I'm talking about a *special* person," she said.

I thought about her remark afterward, and I realized that we have some pretty limited ideas about what makes a person "special" in our lives. If you're feeling sorry for yourself about having no one "special," get out and volunteer some time to people who need you. You'll learn pretty quickly what makes people special in your life.

That's what one woman I spoke with did—although she admitted that it took her awhile to get around to it. "I was very depressed each Christmas after Don died. We didn't have any children and I just felt so sorry for myself. Christmas Day would come and I'd just be numb with sadness, sitting around crying, 'Why me?' After this had been going on for three years I heard about a program my church was sponsoring—a complete turkey dinner for the homeless people in our community. One of the organizers called me and asked if I would be willing to help serve for a couple of hours. I didn't really want to, but I didn't feel right about saying no.

"I went to the church on Christmas and the hall was packed with people. It was a noise riot in there . . . and it didn't smell too good, either. I stood behind the table and started dishing potatoes onto plates as the people went by. I must have stood there for almost an hour before I ever even looked one person in the eye. I was just doing my Christian duty. I didn't want to *know* these people.

"But suddenly something made me look up and I found myself eye to eye with a young woman who was helping her little boy fill a plate. She smiled at me and I was instantly choked with tears. In that moment it sunk in *what this was all about.* For the rest of the day I felt a happiness I hadn't felt in years. I know it sounds corny but I felt like a part of the human race. It was a good feeling. I was never alone on Christmas again."

In my lifetime I've had my special charities—I've done hundreds of speaking engagements for Cerebral Palsy and the American Cancer Society. It's gratifying to contribute time to helping people. It fills up some of the empty space inside. Instead of mourning your loss, say, "I am going to go out and reinvest some of the love my husband gave me by helping others."

Since this seems to be the "me" decade, many charities are hurting for volunteers. You'll be welcomed with open arms wherever you go. There is an endless variety of ways you can volunteer your time, depending on where your interests lie. Here's just a sampling:

- Literacy Volunteers of America: Become a tutor for adults who can't read.
- Hospital auxiliaries: Work in the gift shop, run the book mobile, coordinate fund-raising events.
- Political campaigns: Work the phones, send out mailings, work at the polls on election days (a fabulous way to meet people!).
- Meals on Wheels: Help serve meals to shut-ins.
- Big Sisters programs: Become a big sister (or a "big grandmother," as the case may be) to a child without parents.
- Crisis intervention programs: Work suicide, drug and alcohol hotlines.
- United Fund: In many communities this is the umbrella organization for numerous community services. It's a good place to start if you're not sure what you want to do.
- Women's crisis centers: Work with battered women, victims of rape and other women in crisis situations.
- Church or synagogue: Your church or synagogue offers unlimited opportunities for volunteering your time.

These are just a few ideas. Can you see the range and variety of things you can do? Once you begin to invest time in helping others it will take the focus off your misery and redirect it in positive ways. As a friend who volunteers at a hospital once confided, "I almost feel guilty because I'm getting back so much more than I'm giving."

◈ 8 ◈

Alone and Loving It

"Margery," I said to my friend, "Abe has been gone now for just two months and I know you're grieving and lonely. Maybe it's too soon for you to want to go out and socialize—"

"I couldn't possibly go out," she interrupted. "But I can't bear to be home either. It's so quiet, I'm going crazy."

"I have a suggestion. Why don't you get a pet? It will keep you company and help take your mind off your grief."

Margery took my advice and went to an animal shelter, where she adopted a beautiful plump orange tabby. "It's a wonderful place," she raved. "The animals are so well cared for. And the shelter took the adoption very seriously . . . even checked my credentials."

I was delighted by Margery's buoyant spirits. "What's your darling's name?" I asked.

"His name was Tom when I met him. I had wanted to give him a new name, but they told me it would be quite a trauma for him to undergo a name change at this time."

"Of course," I murmured sympathetically. "I'm so pleased for you, Margery."

I didn't hear from my friend for about three weeks. When she called me, her voice sounded strained to the breaking point.

"What's wrong?" I cried, alarmed.

"Virginia," she said, "I am about to become a murderer. This is the meanest cat I have ever seen. He eats my carpet. He scratches me. He bites me. He regurgitates his meals. He hisses—"

"Margery, you must calm down."

"I haven't slept in weeks," she complained. "My nerves are shot. I tell you, the next time this cat comes near me, I'm going to strangle him with my bare hands."

"Now, now," I said soothingly. "Before you do anything that drastic, why don't you call the shelter. Maybe they'll have a solution."

"I'll have to call them. I'm at my wit's end."

Margery called me back an hour later, sounding more agitated than ever. "I called the shelter and I told them they'd better come and get Tom because I'm about to murder him. The woman on the phone was horrified. She said, 'You can't be serious.'

"I said, 'I'm perfectly serious. I've had it and you'd better come and get this cat because I intend to twist his neck until he's dead.'"

I was listening to this story and falling on the floor laughing. You have to understand that Margery is one of the most gentle, sweetest women I've ever known. It was inconceivable that she could sound so murderous. "So, what happened?" I asked.

"Can you believe this! The woman put me on hold and transferred me to the education department."

"The education department?"

"Don't ask. Anyway, by the time the education department picked up the phone, I was already screaming, 'I don't know who needs to be educated here, but I'm telling you right now that I'm going to kill this cat.'

"The woman's voice on the telephone became very soft. She thought she was dealing with a mental case. I swear, Virginia, there's nothing wrong with me and I resented that. She started telling me about this wonderful cat psychiatrist who might be able to help Tom. Of course, I said, 'You've got to be kidding,' but she was dead serious. She's coming tomorrow, if I don't kill the cat first. Even while I was on the phone, Tom was using my leg for a scratching post. It's unbelievable."

"This is the most fascinating thing I've ever heard," I said. "I wonder what a cat psychiatrist does."

"I have no idea, but I'll tell you one thing. You were right when you said that having a cat would take my mind off my grief." And she hung up.

I was so eager to hear the outcome of this story that I didn't move from my phone the next day. When Margery finally called, she sounded drained but much calmer than she had the day before.

"What happened, Margery? Did she come?"

"Oh, she came, all right," my friend said wearily. "The first thing she asked was, 'Where's the patient?' I'm afraid I snapped at her. I said, '*I'm* the patient. Do you mean

where's the cat? The cat is downstairs destroying my carpet.'

"Then she started asking me all these questions about
whether or not I am a nervous person or have been under
a lot of stress lately. That kind of thing. I was mad. I told
her, 'Yes, I'm under stress. Because of the cat.'

"So then she says, 'I would like to speak with Tom
alone.' I told her to be my guest. I couldn't wait for the
two of them to meet. They deserved each other.

"She was down in the basement with him for almost an
hour and I didn't hear a thing. When she finally came
out, her face was very serious. I did notice that she had a
few runs in her stockings . . . no doubt Tom's work.

"Now, listen to this. She said, 'Tom's a very, very sad
cat.' I asked her what in the world she meant by that, and
she explained that Tom's low self-esteem probably
stemmed from his having had a very sad childhood. She
had his file with her and showed me all the gruesome
details of how Tom had been abandoned by his mother at
an early age."

"Did she tell you what to do?" I asked, enthralled with
the details of this drama.

"Oh, yes, she left full instructions. I'm to put him in
the yard with a hot-water bottle or electric blanket and
feed him catnip. She's coming back next week for a second consultation."

"Margery," I said, "do you mind if I ask you how much
this is costing?"

She choked. "Sixty dollars an hour."

"Amazing," I marveled. "You're paying sixty dollars an
hour to be told your cat has low self-esteem."

"I don't think it's amazing. I think it's insane," she
snapped, and hung up.

I didn't hear from Margery for several weeks, but when

she called again, she sounded almost cheerful.

"You sound great," I told her. "You must have killed the cat."

"You're not going to believe this, Virginia, but Tom has undergone a complete personality change. I don't know what that woman said to him, but whatever it was, it worked."

Margery and Tom ended up becoming great companions. I know his presence eased her loneliness a little.

When the Rooms Are Silent

One of the hardest adjustments to widowhood is how *quiet* everything suddenly is. It is paradoxical that we sometimes even miss a burden. When Harry was ill, at least I had somewhere I had to be. I had things to do, someone who needed me. After he died everything became very empty and silent. How do you fill the emptiness? How do you deal with the silence?

I believe that the only real way to do it is by getting comfortable with yourself. Maybe you've never been alone before—many women move straight from their parents' house to their husband's house. Now it's time to get to know *you*. Take a long hard look at the person you are and want to be and say, "This is a person I'm happy living with."

Unless you make this basic interior adjustment, all your most beloved externals—children, friends, pets— won't distract you from your deep loneliness.

Some men and women move very quickly from widowhood into new marriages—statistically, this is more true for men. Do they do it because they have found true love again . . . or because they can't bear to be alone? I suspect the latter.

And I'll just never get over the kind of subreptilian life-forms we women manage to come across in our search for companionship. An acquaintance, a middle-aged woman, told me about a man she once went to dinner with. It was supposed to be a very casual little meeting. Well, toward the end of the meal, she excused herself to go to the ladies room. When she returned, there was a printed card that the—and I use the term in the loosest form possible—"gentleman" had put at her place. It said: "I've had a vasectomy." The fellow sat there with an insipid, leery grin as she read the card. Imagine, he thought this was a terribly coy, seductive approach!

I tried to picture what I would have done if this had happened to me, and I do believe I would have been speechless for the first time in my life. But my friend handled it in the most wonderful way. She just stood up to leave and, giving him her most withering look, said, "Your father should have had one." Good for her! If I could impart just one piece of wisdom to my fellow widows, it would be this: Don't be so eager to find company that you willingly suffer jerks!

"I'm really torn," a woman once confided to me miserably. "My husband was my whole life, and with him gone, I've felt like half of myself is missing. So why am I so anxious to meet another man? I just don't understand the reason I feel so driven to replace him."

"Maybe you can't bear your own company," I suggested.

She admitted that she hated living by herself. "I still can't get used to shopping for one person. I buy twice as much food as I eat. And I don't enjoy fixing it just for myself."

"Do you like yourself?" I asked boldly.

"I never thought about it. Yes, I suppose I do."

"Think about it," I said. "Think about it a lot. That's your answer."

On the Bright Side

Now, dear readers, let's face a few facts. The truth is, there's a certain delight in living alone and being your own person after you've been part of a couple for many years. And I mean no disloyalty to your dead husbands when I say this. You know how much I loved and depended on Harry. But in many ways I've been given a second chance at life in the past few years as I've discovered just who I am as an individual.

Sometimes it's the little things that provide the most delightful surprises—those mundane day-to-day things that you could never do before and now have the complete freedom to do. For example, I take an absolutely delicious pleasure in talking on the phone, but I'll make a blanket statement: Men hate it when women talk on the phone. I remember how Harry used to come home in the evening and ask, "What's new?" and I'd tell him, "Oh, nothing much." Then I'd get on the phone and talk for two hours and it would drive him crazy. "How come when I ask you what's new, you say nothing, but then you get on the phone and blab for two hours?" he'd demand. It's impossible to explain this to a man, but I'm sure you know exactly what I'm talking about.

I have a friend who calls me when her husband is asleep. He snores so loudly I can hear him long distance. But the minute she says, "Hello, Virginia," he springs to life, completely awake, and starts yelling, "Who are you talking to? Why are you on the phone?" When you're alone, you can talk on the phone to your heart's content and never be afraid of hearing that voice of doom from the other room.

The other thing men hate is when you buy new clothes. Mind you, this has very little to do with economics. They just don't understand it. Men will wear the same suit of clothes for twenty years; for them, clothes are a lifetime investment. I used to buy a new dress and put it in the hall closet behind the coats. Gradually it would work its way to the main closet, and maybe after six months I'd actually wear it. And Harry would notice right away. "Where did you get that?" "This old thing?" I'd ask, all innocence, with the tags hanging down my back. Now I can spend my money to please myself and answer to no one.

Another simple pleasure of living alone is eating ice cream with chocolate sauce in bed at two in the morning without fear of reprisal. And watching T.V. How I love to watch television! Anything and everything. How could I ever justify my goopy taste in movies-of-the-week to another human being?

I am not being facetious about the tremendous grief of losing a loved one. I'm simply urging you to take another look at your own life and needs. Sometimes in a marriage you lose your freedom of choice—about both the big things and the little things. Maybe you don't even see it happening.

I saw an example of this recently when I had guests over for dinner. As invariably happens, the men wanted to leave and the women wanted to stay. As we were talking, one of the husbands suddenly rose to his feet and snapped his fingers, and his wife jumped up off the couch. I looked at him coolly and remarked, "What's wrong with your finger? Did it fall asleep? That happens to me some-times, too. Just shake your wrist." I shook my wrist di-rectly in his face. "See, the blood comes right back." My sarcasm was completely lost on him. He looked straight past me at his wife and said, "Time to go." She went without a word.

I can't stand the way women let themselves be robbed of dignity in this way. But many women have grown so accustomed to abusive behavior that they no longer even question it. Mind you, these long-suffering women often feel drowned in misery when they're finally left all alone. If only they could recall all those times during their mar-riage when they thought, "If only I could get away from him for a few days! If only I didn't have to answer to him every minute. If only I could be my own person for one week."

If you're one of these women, *think*... you now have a chance to recover your dignity and make friends with yourself again.

Create Your Personal Space

The first time I invited a group of friends for dinner at my new apartment, there were gasps of surprise. "This place is so different from the apartment you had with Harry... I just can't believe it," gushed one woman.

"I know." She was right. "I love it, too."

"Didn't you like the old place?"

"Sure I did," I explained. "But that's not me anymore. This is."

Think about it: Have you ever in your life lived in your very own space? Probably not. In the days when we were young it wasn't customary for girls to have their own apartments. We either stayed with our parents until we got married or went away to school. I never even gave much thought to what my own taste was until after Harry died. Our homes were always decorated to conform to our lifestyle and the style of the day.

Harry preferred a comfortable, heavy, masculine look, and the last apartment we shared had thick dark curtains and a very formal air. It was a beautiful place, but with Harry gone I started to feel oppressed by it. For the first time in my life I began to examine what *I* would really like. I became totally obsessed with designing a new apartment for my own pleasure. I never knew it could be so much fun.

My new apartment is light and airy and stuffed with plants and crystal pieces. The walls are lavender and ivory, interrupted by strips of mirror. During the day the sun bounces off the mirrors and makes the rooms shimmer. It is a place of comfort and fun. It perfectly reflects my new lifestyle as a single woman. More important, it sends out the message, I think, that I am a woman secure in my own tastes, willing to express myself in all the details of my home—and not simply waiting around for a new Mr. Right to decorate for.

Of course, not every woman can afford to completely redecorate her home. But I would suggest taking a good look around and asking yourself, "What can I do to make this *my* space?"

When I suggested this once to a friend of mine, she seemed appalled. "I *want* to be reminded of Joe," she protested. "I like the idea of having everything just as it was during our forty years together."

"Sounds like you're making it into a shrine," I observed.

"No, it's not that. But *what will people think* if they see me changing everything around? It'll look like I couldn't wait to get rid of him so I could redecorate."

Ah! There was the heart of the matter. I told her that was the silliest thing I had ever heard her say. But at the same time I understood her feelings. As widows, we sometimes feel we're walking around on eggshells as we keep trying to convince everyone of our deep grief. But sometimes that gets in the way of our starting our lives anew.

It's my contention that the greatest respect you can pay your deceased husband is to go on living. It's certainly what he would have wanted. If you doubt that, just imagine him sitting "up there" listening to you and shaking his head with bemusement. "She won't redecorate because of *me*? But I'm not there anymore . . ."

You may not be aware of how important your living environment is to your mental health, but if you think back to the time when you were happiest in your life, you will probably realize that you also loved the place you lived in—even if it was that cramped little house you bought when you were first married, the one with the leaky roof and dilapidated kitchen appliances.

How did I go about creating my new environment? I started by making a dream list. I wrote down everything I ever wanted: lots of plants (our former apartment was too dark for them), mirrors, hand-painted wallpaper (I chose a floral design), fat cozy couches, a shoe closet that Imelda Marcos would envy . . . and so on. When the apartment was finally remodeled, I nearly cried with the joy of having it. I'll live there the rest of my life, and if some of my friends think it's "a little much," I don't care. It's my home.

Pamper Yourself

Learning to love being alone doesn't happen automatically. You need to work at it. And it won't be an easy task because if you're like most women I know, you probably haven't spent five minutes in the last twenty years thinking about how to please yourself. The very thought may embarrass you. I can hear you saying, "I couldn't be so selfish!" Yes, you can! Now, doesn't it feel good to be selfish for a change?

Think about it this way. When you first got married, you had to get used to living with another person. You had to work at it. It's the same thing now—except that the other person is the self you don't know yet. You have to take the time to discover how to live with that person, too. There are lots of ways to get in touch with your new self.

One friend started keeping a diary after her husband died. She blushed a little when she told me this. "I haven't kept a diary since I was sixteen years old and I felt a little silly about it at first, but I really enjoy it and I never miss a day."

Another woman I know who was widowed in her late seventies spent the last three years of her life (she died at eighty-one) writing her memoirs as a gift to her grandchildren. She wrote them in longhand on lined sheets of paper that she tied together with ribbons. When she finished, there were over four hundred pages, one of the most moving legacies I've ever heard of.

Both of these women learned through their writing how to talk to themselves, how to get in touch with the people they once were and the new individuals they had become. Taking the time for reflection can enrich your personal life. Find the way that works best for you, whether it's writing, gardening, painting or some other activity that is deeply personal. Determine to spend a little time each day engaged in this activity.

Another thing I do is take "Mental Health Days." A Mental Health Day is a day when I turn off my telephone and deliberately reject all interference from the outside. I always come away from these days feeling completely refreshed and rested.

I start off by getting myself glamorous. You may well ask, "What difference does it make how I look when I'm alone?" I feel that glamour isn't something you put on when you're going out. It comes from within and it has to be nurtured. Try it!

Start with a long hot bath accompanied by soft music. Then put on a soft robe that flatters your figure and feels good against your skin. Resist the temptation to think, "Who cares? Who's watching?" Remember that *you're* the one who counts. Then do whatever pleases you. On my Mental Health Day I watch television. I am not ashamed to admit that I *love* television, especially soap operas. Television is like a loyal friend—it's always there and it doesn't talk back. When Donna finally got married on *Another World,* I dressed up and put on makeup to watch it.

I also cook myself an elaborate meal. If you're like me, you tend not to cook for yourself very often. Most people think cooking is worth it only if you're serving someone else. But on this day I cook for myself as if I were my most special company. When I finally go to bed after a day of pampering myself, I really feel wonderful.

A friend of mine has her own variation on the Mental Health Day theme. She goes shopping. "I hit at least three of the best department stores," she says. "I try on perfume and choose a new one. I experiment with makeup. I have lunch..."

"Kind of expensive mental health," I joked when she told me this.

"Oh, Virginia, I don't *buy* anything," she laughed. "I just play." That's the spirit!

Another woman I know works in her garden all day with the radio blasting out the baseball game.

To each her own!

I hope you see my point. When you love yourself, it can transform the experience of being alone from a grim, fearful one to a pleasure that repeats itself every day.

❖ 9 ❖

Living a Golden Life

I may be old (seventy-four years, the last time I
checked), but I'm *good,* darn it—maybe even *better* than I
was a half century ago! A few creaking bones notwith-
standing, I honestly think these are the best years of my
life. I only wish society agreed with me.

In this chapter I want to address those of you who are
seniors, because you're particularly vulnerable at this
stage. In fact, you probably feel like you have three strikes
against you:

1. You're a woman in a male-dominated society.
2. You're a woman *alone* in a world where being a
   couple is considered the only route to happiness.

3. You're an older woman in an age where youth is revered.

And this is the time in your life when you're having to contend with a combination of other problems, too, like illness, a financial squeeze or fears about your ability to protect yourself. Don't these things often get you down? Well, I think it's about time we all stood up and told the world that *we're not going to take it anymore!* After all, we seniors form a substantial percentage of the population— current statistics show that there are some 60 million Americans over the age of fifty. Furthermore, we have the guts, wisdom, expertise and spirit that come with experience. As a group, we are enlightened by long years of coping with the world. Let's figure out how to capitalize on these precious assets! Let's *refuse* to be shunted off into a corner.

To tell you the truth, it scared me to death to get older, at first. I was in television and it's no secret that television is a youth-oriented medium. In fact, when my new cable television program, called *Growing Young*, was turned down by the network in 1984, I was very discouraged. It was to be a talk show co-hosted by me and a delightful man, George Skinner. The management had the gall to give this as their reason for rejection: "What do these senior citizens have to say to anyone? Our audience wants to see young people."

My initial reaction was blind rage. But the rage was followed by a hopelessness, a fear that he was right.

My darling granddaughter cheered me up when she said, "Virginia, you *are* today's woman. If anyone should be on television, it should be you. What does age have to do with it?"

I thought about it and decided that she was right and that never again would I allow myself to be treated with disrespect because of my age.

To the contrary, I'm proud of my age. *Look* at my accomplishments! I've lived into my seventies and I'm still going strong. I know I have a lot left to say and, by God, I'm going to say it.

It all comes down to your state of mind. If you feel old, you will *be* old. If you think life is over, it *will* be over. If you believe the negative comments, they will become *true*.

I get really bugged by the stereotypes of senior citizens. Take television commercials. They always use older people to speak about laxatives and dentures. They're always solemn and sickly—these people do *not* look like fun. I really hit the roof the day I saw a commercial advertising, of all things, adult diapers for older people who are incontinent. Please!

Not long ago I received a call from an advertising agency. They wanted me to do a laxative commercial. "A laxative?" I wrinkled my nose with distaste. Was I so over-the-hill that I was being consigned to the laxative department? I asked, "What exactly would that entail? Excuse the pun."

The humorless young woman on the other end of the line explained, "It will be done in your own words, expressing how you *really feel*."

I said, "Gosh, this is something I've never given serious thought to . . . how I *really feel* about laxatives. But are you aware that my last book was titled *If I Made It, So Can You?*" She didn't laugh. Those laxative people have no sense of humor.

My agent didn't mince words when I told her about the offer. "Virginia, you think you have problems now. If you do a laxative commercial, you couldn't get arrested in Alcatraz. Laxative commercials are for *old* people. It'll make you look over-the-hill."

I agreed. I called the woman back and said, "No thanks . . . but please call me if you have something with a younger flavor. I'm really the Pepsi generation, my dear."

"The old gray mare, she ain't what she used to be," quoted a friend of mine recently. "Face it, Virginia, it's about time we slowed down a bit." (She was appalled after hearing that I had just walked forty blocks to a restaurant, eschewing my usual taxi.)

"I agree," was my response. "This old gray mare is *better* than she used to be—and she isn't even gray, thanks to Clairol."

When *The Golden Girls* became a hit television series, I was thrilled. When Clara Peller became the hottest property in advertising, I cried, "It's about time!" I'm filled with admiration for women like Lady Bird Johnson, Kitty Carlisle, Helen Hayes and Betty Ford. I dance with delight when I see Elizabeth Taylor, radiant and secure. These women have chosen to ignore the dictate that they are too old to be beautiful or successful. Too old to make brand-new contributions. They clearly take joy in life.

The most destructive words in the world are "I'm too old to do that." They are destructive to your self-esteem, your initiative, your forward momentum.

Growing Younger

My friend Ruby called me one day to announce she was moving to Florida. "Why, that's wonderful," I told her. I was delighted that she was getting out of her rut—until she told me the reason.

"It's about time I slowed down a little," she said. "I'm

too old to live in this crazy city. It's too dangerous. I just want to finish my days in peace."

"What the hell are you talking about?" I asked. "Ruby, you're only sixty years old. And you're in good health. When you talk about the rest of your days, you're talking about a good twenty-five years!"

"My daughter thinks it's a good idea."

"Your daughter is an idiot—she gave you a funeral plot for your birthday."

"She means well."

"Ruby, listen. If you were moving to Florida because you thought you would be happy there, fine. I'd be all for it. But if you're putting yourself out to pasture at your age, you'll be dead in five years instead of twenty-five."

She was offended by my frank remarks—and she did move to Florida. But a funny thing happened on her way to the pasture.

She called me about three months after the move and her voice was filled with excitement. "I'm having the time of my life down here," she said. "I've never been so busy. There are clubs... I've met a man... we go sailing together. Can you imagine me, the original city girl, going sailing? It's wonderful."

"I'm surprised to hear this, Ruby," I teased her. "I thought you were too old for that kind of stuff."

"So did I. But I was wrong. I feel a good ten years younger these days. You should see my tan."

Good for Ruby. I sighed with relief.

In his book *Life Begins at Sixty*, Bill Case makes this statement: "Personally, I believe that life begins when I first open my eyes every morning. Something like a watch you wind every day. So maybe you can go along with me when I say, 'Life begins at sixty or seventy or whenever you become determined enough to say it should.'"

And the delightful Helen Hayes, in her book *Our Best Years*, tells this story: "On a recent trip to California, I had a bit of sciatica to cope with. My friends rushed me off to a doctor. The doctor wanted to rush me off to the hospital. But me, I hustled down to the airport and flew home. There, of course, I went to bed for a nice, therapeutic rest. The decisions were all mine and I was satisfied. The only one that gave me a bit of a problem was the decision to *get up again*. You know how it is; there comes a time when you really have to say, 'Get up, old girl,' or you run the risk of making bed your habitat."

"Get up, old girl." It's a good exhortation. On those days when you feel ready to give up and sink into a state of sedate senior citizenship, look at yourself in the mirror and say, "Get up, old girl."

A woman I know once said to me, "It's very odd, Virginia, but I actually feel younger now at sixty-eight than I felt at twenty-five."

"How so?"

"I'm relaxed, for one thing. With four kids to raise, I used to feel harried and exhausted most of the time. Then, when I finally got the kids raised, Jim got sick and I was busy nursing him. And my own mother was ill and I had to watch out for her. I felt like a wreck most of the time. The way I see it, these are *my* years. I'm having fun, I'm being silly, I'm going where I want to go and doing what I want to do. And when the children disapprove, I tell them to mind their own business."

Her words made me think about my own life, and I realized that in some ways the same thing was true for me. A marvelous freedom has come with my older years —a breath of fresh air that I never experienced when I was younger.

Can we really grow younger with age? It's a strange

thought, isn't it, but well worth examining. I've known many older women who seem to sparkle with age. And I think I can tell you what qualities set these women apart:

- They view their cups as being half full, not half empty. They are emphatically *not* just waiting to die.
- They take advantage of their new freedom to have adventures, instead of mourning their lost youth.
- They focus on the future, not the past.
- They don't take life too seriously. They're always ready for laughter.
- They put the wisdom of their years to use instead of treating it as unimportant.
- They believe beauty is possible at any age.
- They see this stage of their lives as a new phase, not a bad phase.
- They live their lives one day and one experience at a time.
- They are delighted to be alive and thank God daily for the gift of life.

If you don't recognize yourself in this picture, it's time to take serious stock of your life and your attitudes.

Facing Real Issues

At lunch one day, I was expounding (as usual) on my views about growing older, when my friend Gloria stopped me. "It's easy for you to say that, Virginia. But how many older women are going to identify with you? You have enough money to do anything you like. There's a car service that picks you up and takes you everywhere. Your speaking engagements give you a chance to travel. You have more dinner invitations than you can accept. The life of a celebrity is a far cry from the life of an ordinary woman in America."

"You've got a point," I said. "But the bottom line is that celebrities have to deal with age and loneliness just like everyone else."

"Maybe. But I'd say it's easier to be old and rich than it is to be old and poor."

I'm hardly rich, but I realized that she was right about what she said. Although I believe that all the money and fame in the world can't replace basic self-esteem, I also know that many older women face a myriad of very real obstacles to happiness and comfort. Some of these may be true for you. Among them are

- Declining health and poor physical fitness that limit your mobility and freedom
- Tight financial times, especially if you're forced to make do on a Social Security paycheck
- Vulnerability on the street: being an easy target for muggers and con artists and being forced to take public transportation out of financial necessity
- Inadequate preparation for handling the ins and outs of life alone: not knowing how to get home repairs done, how to make financial decisions, how to avoid getting "ripped off"
- Losing companions and close friends through illness or death.

These are very real issues, and they are not to be taken lightly. I can't tell you that life is all roses at seventy-four, and I want to address the true concerns of senior citizens with respect. But the good news is that there are many services available to help you. You don't have to be stoic. You're not alone.

Recently I read an item about a service sponsored by Harvard Medical School called the Widowed-to-Widowed Program. The service uses widows to counsel other widows and help them get over the initial hump of their loss. I was very impressed to learn of this supportive program, and I realized that if you know where to look for help, there's never any need for you to feel alone, vulnerable or put-on-the-shelf.

I'm going to take a few moments here to give you some resources that can help you. These are people you can call, organizations of seniors that you can become involved with. Sure, your situation is unique and your needs are special. But I'll bet there is something here for you.

- American Association of Retired Persons. The main office is located in Washington, D.C. (call 202-872-4700). This is a great source of information if you're looking for specific services. You can also subscribe to the association's magazine, *Modern Maturity* or the *AARP News Bulletin*.
- The National Association of Senior Citizens. The office is located in Arlington, Virginia (phone 703-241-1533). Subscribe to two wonderful publications, *Senior Guardian* and *Our Age*.
- Gray Panthers. Surely you've heard of this marvelous group that has taken up the banner on behalf of senior citizens. They can help you with a wide range of problems—and if you choose to join the club, so to speak, you may find rich rewards. Their main office is located in Philadelphia, Pennsylvania (phone 215-382-3300). They also publish *The Network Newsletter*.

- National Council of Senior Citizens. This organization, also located in Washington, D.C. (phone 202-347-8800) publishes *Senior Citizens News,* a monthly publication.
- Association of Volunteer Bureaus. This is a clearing house for volunteer organizations, located in Norfolk, Virginia. You might also contact the Commission on Voluntary Service and Action in New York, N.Y.
- VISTA/Peace Corps. If you really want to throw your hat into the involvement ring, VISTA and the Peace Corps provide rewarding (and rigorous) opportunities. Both organizations are located in Washington, D.C.
- Institutes for Lifetime Learning, in affiliation with the AARP in Washington, D.C., provides educational opportunities for seniors.

Check your local Yellow Pages for the services and organizations in your area.

Shattering the Myths

I've noticed that being a senior citizen sometimes feels a lot like being a child again. Everyone's always saying, "No, you can't do that... you're not allowed." But that simply is not true. There's no reason you can't do anything if your health is good. Don't believe that some of the great joys in life are unavailable to you just because you're older.

I know a businessman who goes out of his way to hire senior citizens to work in his store. Why? "They're better, more reliable workers... and nicer to the customers.

These young kids don't seem to care."

I heard of a book publisher who hires older people for his sales force. "I've got more than a hundred and fifty years' worth of experience on my team," he says proudly.

Maybe it would make society more comfortable if we'd keep in our places—or what they've told us our places are. They like to think of us at home, spending a quiet day in the garden, not making any waves.

A friend of mine laughed when she told me, "My daughter is so disgusted with me. She suspects my male friend and I are having sex, and she can't contain her disapproval. She says, 'Mother, you're seventy-five years old, for goodness' sake.'"

"Well, our children don't approve of us having sex at any age—except, of course, on the single occasion that produced them," I observed. "What do you tell her?"

"To mind her own business, of course."

"Good for you."

"Not that she will. It irritates me that she treats me as if I don't know my own mind."

Let's look at some of the myths about growing old. Once you recognize that they are only myths, you can simply laugh them away and refuse to live a life that's bound by them.

MYTH NUMBER ONE: The older you get, the more senile you become. You lose your memory, your common sense and your intelligence.

I once knew an eighty-two-year-old woman whose friends were concerned about her because they felt her mind was slipping. She just didn't seem as sharp anymore, and her mind always seemed to be wandering. In conversations, half the time she didn't seem to understand what was being said. Her family was getting ready to give up on her when they sent her to the doctor for a checkup. He discovered that the problem was not that she didn't understand what was being said, but that she couldn't *hear* what was being said. He set her up with a hearing aid and she was her old self again, just like that.

The myth about losing memory is just nonsense. I, for one, remember practically everything anyone's ever said to me. I have a friend who remembers the names of people she went to elementary school with—she's eighty-four. Incidentally, her granddaughter, who is twenty-two, can't do the same.

MYTH NUMBER TWO: Older people are set in their ways, humorless and bound by tradition.

Over the years I've met so many men and women who don't fit this mold. My older friends are not dour, "cross" people. They tell sidesplitting jokes, occasionally off-color. They enjoy taking firm stands on issues and getting involved in controversy because they know they have nothing to lose!

I was walking in Central Park recently when I noticed a woman who was passing out leaflets. She was at least eighty, frail and tiny, but there was a sparkle in her eye as she explained to me how necessary it was for us to halt the nuclear threat. "We must do this for the children," she said with deep conviction.

I asked her why she was standing in the hot sun on a Sunday afternoon to pass out leaflets. "Because I believe in it," she said simply. "Don't you think that if we believe in a cause, we should be willing to work for it?"

Indeed I do!

MYTH NUMBER THREE: Physical fitness doesn't pertain to anyone over sixty. I'll admit that the old machine needs repairs more often than it used to. But we can be physically fit. I know seniors who run in marathons . . . play tennis . . . bicycle twenty miles a day.

Part of the myth is that if you exercise, you run the risk of having a heart attack or breaking a hip. Better safe than sorry, right?

Not necessarily. Physical fitness is a very individual thing, and current studies about longevity recommend some exercise. If your doctor says you can do it, go for it. The joints might creak a little. Maybe you'll have to buy Ben-Gay by the gross. But a lot of the fears you may have about what might happen to you if you exercise are unfounded.

MYTH NUMBER FOUR: Forget sex after sixty. This is one of the biggest myths, and I suspect it came about because sex and romance are considered to be occupations of the young. I don't think these young folks can bear the idea of oldies having intimate relations. They think it's undignified. To the contrary, it is very dignified, because sex is a wonderful and natural part of life—we're not going to let them take it away from us!

MYTH NUMBER FIVE: Senior citizens are in "the twilight of their lives." Sundown is just around the corner. People expect us to live as though we have one foot already in the grave.

A seventy-eight-year-old woman told me this story. "I was mentioning to my daughter that I'd like to move to Arizona, but I wasn't ready to do it yet. I told her maybe I'd move in five years. She looked startled, and suddenly I realized that she didn't think I should be planning that far ahead, that maybe I didn't have five years left. I thought,

'Yes, maybe that's true, but I'm certainly not going to base the rest of my life on that fear.'"

There are other myths, large and small, that show up in our lives every day. We can choose to believe them or we can ignore them . . . it's entirely up to us.

In your "golden years," you can kick up a storm or you can stop kicking. You can let the world know you're alive or you can hide in the background. Which is it going to be for you?

❖ *10* ❖

"Table for One, Please"

I want you to imagine two scenes. The first takes place on a lovely summer evening. You are sitting in your home feeling cramped and restless. You'd like to be out among people, but all your friends are busy. The thought flashes across your mind, as it has so many times, that if only your husband were alive, you would be enjoying dinner in a bright, busy restaurant, surrounded by fun people and noisy laughter. But now that's out of the question. You're alone. So, once again you resign yourself to sitting at home wishing for the things you can no longer have.

Now imagine a different scene. It is the same evening, and instead of staying home, you say to yourself, "What the heck. I'm going out." You make a reservation at an old-favorite restaurant and take a lot of time getting ready, putting on your prettiest summer dress. No, you've never done this before, but *why not?*

When you enter the restaurant, you're feeling a little nervous. As you say to the maître d', "Table for one, please," you imagine all the diners turning to look at you. "Oh, how sad," you imagine them whispering. "Where are her children? Doesn't she have friends?"

But you press on. You're seated at a nice, small table. You order a glass of wine, sit back, relax, look around you, take in the scene. It's been a long time since you've been here and you really love this restaurant.

And suddenly, in the midst of your reverie, you reach a startling conclusion: *It's perfectly okay to be here alone at your table for one!* Nobody is looking at you strangely. You're really enjoying yourself. You are downright proud of yourself for making this dramatic statement of independence. You make a toast to yourself. You've made it!

I believe that having the security to go out alone is the greatest sign that a widow has finally accepted herself and her life. It may seem like a small thing, but it's not. It's a very courageous act. I learned this lesson myself not long after Harry died. To be honest with you, at that time I wouldn't have dreamed of going out to a restaurant alone. But I knew a widow then who was a very popular and well-connected woman. Her husband had been an important man in business, and descriptions of her lavish dinner parties filled the society pages.

Then I began running into her at a New York restaurant I frequented. Curiously, I always found her dining alone. I'm ashamed to confess that when I saw her I thought, "What terrible thing could have happened for this lovely woman to have lost her social life?"

Finally, I went over to her table one night and said, "Mary, I must ask you something. I've seen you having dinner alone here many times. You never look uncomfortable—you don't bother pretending that you're waiting for someone. I just can't understand why you eat here alone when you could be with all your friends."

Her answer was very direct. "I'm not invited out every single night and I hate to sit in my dining room alone, so I come here to be around people."

I must say really admired her guts. Now, you'd think I, of all people, would have enough self-esteem to do the same thing, but it took me a long time to get up the courage. For years, even when I traveled to strange cities, I'd refuse to go alone to hotel dining rooms. I'd order room service and hide out in my room.

After talking to Mary, though, I began to think about it, and on my next trip I checked into my room and had a little talk with myself. I said, "It's very lonely up here and there's a lovely dining room downstairs. I'm going to pull myself together and I'm going to go downstairs and have a pleasant evening." And that's what I did. I had to force myself that first time, but now I feel totally comfortable dining alone. It's become a good time for me to think, to make lists for myself of things I must do, to work on speeches—all the busy little things I don't like attending to in the quiet of my own home.

A novelist friend of mine once told me she gets lots of good ideas for her plots and characters from overhearing the conversations of people seated around her in restaurants. She even carries a little mirror so that while checking her lipstick, she can match the voice behind her to a face!

Be a Somebody

But I'm still left wondering why so many women don't make an effort to fight their loneliness and unhappiness. Often, it seems, we actually *choose* unhappiness. A woman confided to me one day that she was getting married again, to a man who was very different from her first husband. "My friends tell me that this is my chance to become a new woman," she said, laughing. "They say I've got to forget about the life I led with my first husband."

"But why would you have to?" I asked.

"Well," she explained, "I was married for many years to a man who was an outdoorsman and I loved the outdoors, too. We used to go fishing and camping together all the time."

"Doesn't the man you're marrying share your interests?"

She said, "He *hates* the outdoors. Jim prefers the theater and the ballet."

"What *do* you have in common?"

"Not much, really." She shrugged. "But my friends say it doesn't matter and I agree with them. I'm convinced that great love comes only once in a lifetime. I had it with my first husband. I can't expect to find the same happiness twice."

"I have news for you," I replied vehemently. "You are fully entitled to more than one great love. You just haven't given yourself a chance to find another real love."

If there's one thing I hate, it's seeing women settle for second (or third or fourth) best because they don't believe they deserve real happiness—and then making up convoluted excuses to justify their compromises. I know plenty of people whose second marriages were *much* happier than their first and it has nothing to do with what they deserved!

So now I said to this woman, "I have some advice for you, and you may not want to hear this, but you should always go out with someone you have a lot in common with. At a certain stage in your life, unless you have those mutual interests, the time you spend with your husband will be pure torture."

But I wonder *why* women insist on feeling guilty about being happy again after their husbands are dead. Many women feel it's somehow wrong to love more than once, to enjoy a man's company after their husband dies, to feel good about their lives the second time around. Why feel guilty because you want to continue to enjoy life? Why be embarrassed to admit that more than one man can make you happy? Every widow should ask herself this: Would my husband have wanted me to throw myself into his grave so we could be buried together forever? Or would he have wanted me to carry on, learning, growing, making friends, expressing my love—all the wonderful things we shared in our time?

Recently, during a question-and-answer session after one of my speeches, a woman got up and asked a personal question completely unrelated to my topic: "How long, Virginia, did you mourn Harry? I have a friend who is just inconsolable about her husband's death."

"There are some people who never seem to get over it," I answered. "When we lose someone we love, a piece of us dies with that person. But we're all given the gift of innumerable choices of how to live richly rewarding and happy lives. And, you know, you can allow all the good qualities of your husband—his warmth, his love—to live on if you *choose* happiness."

I believe this with all my heart. But it doesn't necessarily come naturally. In a sense, learning to live and be happy again is just like learning to do anything else. For example, my friend Sarah is a fabulous cook, the best I know. But when she got married she couldn't even boil water. She threw herself into the effort of learning and perfecting and *showing off* three times a day because her friends and family had to eat and she wanted the best for them. Similarly, the new widow must decide to go on living after her husband's death—and then decide to live *well* and *happily.* It's just as simple as that.

Of course, you can also just sit back and say, "It's too late. I'm too old. Who cares?" But I think that when you care about yourself, you are opening the door for others to show that they care. And *that,* if you haven't noticed, is what makes this world go around!

Now, some of us wouldn't have quite so much to recover from after the deaths of our husbands if we owned up, in our midnight confessions, to the fact that our marriages weren't exactly all we'd once hoped they would be. Are you shocked? I'll go one step further. My darling Harry made our marriage a little less than heavenly because he drank frequently and sometimes he drank to excess. There, I've said it. I loved Harry throughout the years we were married, and I cherish his memory, but I can understand why, for some women, widowhood feels like a release.

I know a woman in her seventies who, in the years since her husband died, has absolutely glowed. She looks more and more marvelous. One day she remarked, "Virginia, these are the best years of my life."

I was surprised. Her life with her husband, an important politico, had appeared—very publicly—to be glamorous, stable, enviably happy. "Come on," I joked. "That's like an asthmatic who takes a decent breath every now and then saying, 'What a wonderful thing to breathe.'"

"You hit on the right analogy," she said, nodding. "I suffered thirty-five years with awful asthma and now I can breathe."

"I was only kidding!" I cried. "What do you mean?"

"You never knew about this, but life with my husband was not easy. You know, his career took him away from home constantly, which wasn't so bad. But I think he saw other women, too . . . there were little clues, like the times he'd go out campaigning when there wasn't an election. I endured it all my life and finally I'm free." Lee Hart, take note!

Another woman said to me, not entirely in jest, "When my husband died, I had the locks changed. I was afraid he'd come back."

Widowhood, my friends, can be an important time of self-revelation for you. Be honest. Maybe what you miss is the burden of your marriage, not the joy. Maybe you're only mourning the loss of predictability. Freedom can come as a great shock!

Many women have the idea that after a certain age nothing new will ever again happen to them. But just the opposite is true. There's something new waiting for you every day of your life, if you'll only embrace it.

That doesn't mean there won't be some tough adjustments. There will come a time when you'll have to make a new set of friends who share your experiences. It may be lousy to discover that your lifelong friends aren't soul mates anymore, simply because they're still in couples and you're single. You may feel that they're distancing themselves from you because they want an even number of friends. It happens sometimes and you musn't waste yourself on being bitter about it. And don't tell me you're too old to make new friends because I'm seventy-four and I've made a couple of the best friends of my life during the past five years.

Now, if you think all of this is easy for me to say, you should know the truth. There was never anyone who had less self-esteem than I had. I used to feel that I had to make people laugh or they wouldn't like me. I was too often overly generous in an attempt to buy my friendships. I guess I didn't believe I had enough inside myself that people would want.

I've had to do plenty of soul-searching about that. I'm opening up my heart now to tell you that this woman you see who seems so strong and self-assured was at one time a very shy and frightened person who didn't think she was as good as everyone else. Only during the past five years have I slowly come to the realization that I am worthy of success and happiness.

Happiness requires real courage. I find it funny that I had to wait until I was seventy to learn about bravery. Many years ago, when I had my television show, there was nothing I wouldn't do for the cameras. I rode a donkey. That was a snap, so I tried an elephant. A piece of cake. My producer once booked an Indian knife thrower who was scheduled to throw eight knives at a female volunteer from the audience. *I* volunteered. I didn't bat an eye as eight knives flew around my body.

Now, though, I understand what real courage is. Sometimes courage means being able to cry and admit your weakness. I've finally learned how to cry. And how to muster the guts to accept happiness. Somehow, I'll admit, it's been impossible to imagine that I could turn my life around 180 degrees in my later years.

How much can you really change? Many think that we

only get more set in our ways as we get older and that all our good and bad qualities just get magnified as time goes on. That's nonsense. I've changed a lot since Harry died. Some of my friends think I've just become more difficult and eccentric, but for me the road to healing has included making my own choices, regardless of the opinions of others. I only have time these days for people who wish me well. I want build-uppers around me, not tear-downers.

Attitude is everything—the God-given gift within all of us that helps us to survive. Some suggest I have *too much* attitude. And the older I get, the more attitude I seem to have! Perhaps I'm not as tactful as I once was—yes, believe it or not, I was once very tactful! Now I will not tolerate negative comments or insults. If someone makes an insulting remark to me, I'll immediately retort, "Why would you *say* such a thing?" Before, I might have just shrugged it off or laughed, too insecure to stick up for myself. No more!

Knowing You're Healed

How do you know when you've crossed the bridge... when you've survived to emerge from the pain a new person? What are the signs? What does "Wonderful Widowhood" look like? Let me share with you some of the signs that will indicate that you've made peace with your grief and are really living a full life as a wonderful older woman.

SIGN NUMBER ONE: You're no longer a worrywart. My father always said to me, "Worry is interest on trouble before it's due." Worry stops your happiness dead in its tracks. I have a friend who thrives on it. Such paranoia I've never seen! If you look at her the wrong way, she'll call you later and say, "You were acting a little strange today. Did I do something to offend you?"

Once, when she pulled this routine on me for the hundredth time, I said, "Yes! Yes, you did. Everything was fine until you made this phone call."

She's the same way with men—except maybe worse. For five years this woman has been going out with the same man and they clearly have a solid relationship. But she prefers to torture herself.

She called me one day and announced with absolute certainty, "I don't think I'm ever going to see him again."

Had I not known her so well, I might have been alarmed. But I just sighed. "Why not?"

"Well," she said indignantly, "he was supposed to call me this morning and when he didn't call by noon, I called him—and do you know what he said?"

"What did he say?"

Her voice rose to a near shriek. "He said, 'I can't talk to you right now.'"

"That's it? That's the reason you're cutting off a five-year relationship?" I couldn't believe it.

"Don't you see, Virginia," she insisted, "he probably had another woman there. What other excuse could he have for not talking to me?"

I could think of at least a dozen, but I realized it was pointless to argue. Some people need to be anxious about something all the time. Perhaps they think that if they worry about a hundred little things, then the big worries will stay in the background. I don't know. I don't think it's ever too late to get professional help! My advice is:

Don't let the past eat away at you. And don't agonize over problems you think you might have in the future. Make the best of *now* and *make* your good fortune happen!

SIGN NUMBER TWO: You stop blaming your husband for dying. When a woman first confided in me how furious she was with her husband for dying—three years after his death—it took me by surprise. After all, it wasn't *his* idea. But I have found the reaction a fairly common one. Many women fell cheated by the death of their partner. The children are finally grown, the bills are paid, retirement is due—these were supposed to be their golden years together. Then he died.

But anger won't help a thing. It will rob you of the rest of your life. While it's normal to feel some resentment at the apparent injustice of it, it's a phase every widow goes through. Time will heal this. And when those angry feelings soften, you'll know you're going to be okay.

SIGN NUMBER THREE: You exorcise your husband's ghost. For the first couple of years after Harry died, I felt he was with me every day—and I mean that literally. I was convinced his ghost was lurking around my apartment to bedevil me, hiding my jewelry, interrupting my dreams, rattling my windows at night. I'd say to him, "Harry, I want to sleep tonight. Where did you put my gold ring?"

It was driving me crazy. I wanted to get on with my life, but Harry's presence was so strong. When I moved to a new apartment, he followed me there.

Finally, in desperation, I went to a psychic friend of mine. "Kenny," I implored, "every night Harry roams my apartment. I want him to rest. I'm afraid that his soul is disturbed . . . and God knows mine is!"

Kenny answered, "There is only one way to release him. You must get non-iodized salt and go around your house and shake it into every single corner of every single room. Don't forget even one corner or it won't work. Then, when you've done that, you must go out into the hall and throw salt on your door."

So there I was, standing in the hallway of my building with a salt shaker, furiously throwing salt at my door, when my neighbor came by.

"Virginia, what *are* you doing?"

I stopped shaking and, trying to cover my embarrassment, said quickly, "Oh, I'm just experimenting with a new insecticide."

Her face registered alarm. "Does the building have bugs?"

"No, no," I assured her. "Just me. I have bugs."

"Oh, my God, I'd better call the super. If you have bugs, then we'll all have them. We'd better get an exterminator in here."

I tried again. "No, I don't actually have bugs *yet*. I'm just trying this out in case I ever get bugs. You can't be too careful."

She went away, convinced I was nuts.

I laugh whenever I think of this, but I'm serious when I say that you have to release your husband's ghost for the sake of your own mental health. When you think of him with love, but let him go, you'll be able to move on.

SIGN NUMBER FOUR: Your amnesia is cured. Many widows suffer from amnesia. A recently widowed woman once said to me, with panic in her voice, "I'm just scared to death. I don't even remember who I was before I was married."

I answered, "I'll tell you who you were. You were a very

popular girl. You came from a fine family who gave you a good education. You were charming. You loved to paint and make pottery."

She looked at me, astounded. "I don't remember any of that! It's been years since I've thought of painting."

I told her, "It's a beautiful thing to merge your identity with your husband's as the two of you share your lives. But at what stage in your marriage did you totally disappear so that now you can't remember who you were before you met him?"

We so easily slip into defining ourselves in the context of our marriages. When asked, "Who are you?" we answer easily, "I'm a wife. I'm a mother." Now it's time to get back in touch with ourselves as individuals.

I know a very talented jewelry designer. She's in her early seventies and she only started her business ten years ago. "This is something I always wanted to do," she told me. "But I put it off for most of my life. At first I thought I would wait until the children were grown. And then other things became priorities. I forgot about it. When Richard died I was very lonely and bored. But one day I remembered my early ambition. I couldn't believe I had forgotten it my whole life."

Now is the time to brush the cobwebs off your dreams and begin making them come true.

SIGN NUMBER FIVE: You get your vinegar back. If you suffer from low self-esteem and insecurity, you probably let people walk all over you. Your children direct your life. Your friends run your social calendar. You allow men to treat you with disrespect. You accept abuse from store clerks and government offices and airlines and car dealers and taxi drivers.

As women, we were all conditioned never to "make

waves," to be peacemakers rather than fighters. In our efforts to measure up to this ideal we've all let a lot of things go by in life. It's hard to stand up for yourself when you've never learned how.

Now you are a widow. You are an older woman. Two strikes against you, some people would say. I disagree. Two strikes in your favor is more like it!

Make it a practice to speak your mind. You don't have to be obnoxious . . . just let people know that they're dealing with a real, live, kicking human being.

I know a widow who kept her mouth shut for two years while her son made virtually every arrangement for her. He paid her bills, he hired her help, he mowed her lawn. "I'm surprised he didn't follow me into the bathroom," she recalled. At one point he decided that she needed to sell the house where she had lived for thirty years. "He had a nice little one-bedroom condo all picked out," she told me, "and he took me to look at it.

"While he was busy raving about how happy I'd be there, I stood and listened, perfectly miserable. It was a *box*. It was horrible. I hated it. I wanted to keep the house. And suddenly something in me snapped. I said, '*No.'*

"My son looked like a bolt of lightning had struck him, but I felt marvelous, almost giddy. It was the first time I had spoken my mind and refused to be led around like a dog on a leash."

SIGN NUMBER SIX: You have fun with yourself. I find ways to entertain myself that are kind of nutty. For example, the incinerator in my building is down the hall, just one apartment away, and I get the greatest charge out of rushing down the hall to throw my trash out—*dressed only in a flimsy nightgown.* You're probably wondering why I don't put on a robe, but there's something about this risky little deed that gives me great excitement. I open my door, stick my head out into the hall, and look first to the right, then to the left. If the coast is clear, I run down the hall, my nightgown flying, throw the trash out and race back. I slam the door shut behind me, take a deep breath, and say, "Thank God, I made it!"

Once I was almost caught by my neighbor's husband. As I started to return from the incinerator room, I saw him standing by the elevator. I shrank down, my heart pounding, and hid there until he left.

What makes this routine particularly eccentric is that I do it several times a day. I have a fetish about having things in my wastebaskets. If there's even a scrap of paper, I feel compelled to empty the basket.

This little game thrills me—it's like having a clandestine love affair. Isn't that the craziest thing you've ever heard of? When I'm racing down the hall in my nightgown to throw away *a* piece of Kleenex or *a* paper towel, I say to myself, "Virginia, you're nuts!"

And I don't care. I'd rather be nuts than a dead fish. I love the fact that at the age of seventy-four I can still collapse into peals of giggles over the silliest things.

Get Busy and Live!

Life is just too precious to let it slip by while we're feeling sorry for ourselves. I have my low moments, to be sure, but most of the time I am just bursting with the realization of how great and full my life has been—what a wonderful, priceless gift it is. I think I really discovered this when I had cancer. That's a heck of a way to learn a lesson about life, but I'm grateful for it. When I wrote

There Goes What's Her Name in 1965, people didn't talk frankly about cancer—it was a horrible mystery. I had never imagined that cancer could happen to me, any more than I imagined I would ever have gray hair or dentures or become a widow. I took life for granted.

After my surgery I refused to talk about it for a long time. It embarrassed me that I could be so vulnerable, and I was bitter that this had happened to me. It seemed so unfair.

But one day I was doing an arthritis telethon with Milton Berle. The money wasn't coming in and we were getting increasingly discouraged. Finally I found myself worked into such a state of emotion that I faced the audience and said, "This morning I looked at myself in the mirror and I said to myself, 'Four years ago the doctor told me I had less than a year to live.'" A sudden hush came over the studio audience as I said these words. It was a breathless moment.

I continued, "Thinking that I had only a little time left, I asked myself, 'What am I going to do?' I knew I was sitting on a time bomb and I realized how precious every single moment of my life was.

"Today, listening to the inspirational stories, I found myself stretching my fingers and thinking about how terrible it would be if I couldn't do that. I look at these brave, wonderful people who can't even tie their shoelaces or brush their teeth, people who are in agonizing pain every day of their lives—but they're smiling as they ask for money. And all we have to do is go to our phones, use our dialing fingers, and give.

"Why aren't we giving? Why don't we see what a tremendous gift life is?"

I spoke these words from the heart, and it was a great moment of realization for me. I knew in that instant that

I wanted to live fully every minute that I had and never stop being thrilled to have the gift of life—even when times were the hardest.

There is a wonderful inspirational book written by that remarkable senior citizen Helen Hayes. It's called *Our Best Years* and I urge you to read it. One of the passages in this book really hit home for me and it sums up best what all of us should understand as we go forward in this new phase of our lives:

> Sometimes older people sound off about the good old days as though nothing today were worthwhile. Actually, those olden days were good mostly because we weren't—so old, or so good. Other oldsters fear ridicule and, therefore, they retreat. But, as James Thurber once said, "You might as well fall flat on your face as lean too far over backwards."

So I invite you to take off your blinders and see the wonderful opportunity that your life is today. Reach out and be a part of the world.

For myself, I fully expect to be around kicking up a storm for some time to come. Join me in the adventure!

◈ *11* ◈

Questions from the Floor

In the more than thirty years that I have been in
television and on the speaker's circuit, I have fielded
thousands of questions from audiences.

Are you familiar with the old saying that there are only
thirty-six original ideas in the world? That's the way I feel
about the questions I hear from women all over America.
It doesn't matter whether I'm speaking to a group of sophisticated women in an urban department store or I'm at
a town hall meeting on a back road in Middle America—
the questions are essentially the same.

This underscores my belief that in spite of the varying
trappings of our lives, we're all much the same under-
neath. So, what *do* women really care about?

They care about giving and receiving love. They care about making a worthwhile contribution to their communities. They care about their own sense of pride and self-worth. They care about living their lives with a degree of independence. They care about raising their children to be honest, good, concerned human beings. They care about making every minute of their lives count. They care about sharing themselves with others in the most meaningful way possible.

And what do women fear? They fear themselves, most of all. They fear that they won't be able to find the inner resources that will carry them through the hard times. Many women have lived their lives hearing others tell them, "You're a woman . . . you're weak . . . you can't handle this alone." They begin to believe it's true. They forget how to trust their own inner voices.

In the past year, as I've been writing this book, I have talked a great deal on my speaking engagements about being a widow. I'd like to share with you a composite view of the questions women have asked me and my answers. Chances are, these are *your* questions, too.

If you have concerns that *haven't* been addressed in this book, I hope you'll write to me in care of my publisher, Simon and Schuster. I want you to know that I have a great deal of concern and regard for you. As women, we share a common bond, and I would be delighted to hear from you.

Now, on to the questions . . .

When does grief end?

Real grief never ends. In a small corner of your heart, you carry the pain of your loss around with you all your life. That's hard to face, isn't it? But you *do* learn to live with it, and the expression of grief ends naturally if you are truly intent upon living. You will probably begin to heal after a year because that's when you stop thinking, "Last year at this time we did this..." But the period of grieving changes with each individual, and I can't give you firm guidelines about when yours will end. It's like my friend with pneumonia who asked me, "Virginia, how long before I'll be better?"

I said, "How can I possibly know? I'm not in your body. You should go out when you feel well enough. It might be tomorrow and it might be two months from now."

Can I really be happy without a man?

Most women think they need a man in their lives, but wanting a man and *needing* one are two different things.

I think you have to ask yourself *why* you think you can't be happy without a man. Is there a big hole in your life when a man isn't around? Do you feel less of a person? You know, many women lose their identities to their men —at great cost to themselves. I remember a woman who once said to me with some pride, "My husband and I don't need other people in our lives. We do everything together. We're everything to each other." I thought, "Boy, is she in for trouble when he dies!" If you place your happiness completely in the hands of another person, you are in for real trouble. Never forget that you can only express true love if you love yourself first.

Can I adjust sexually to a new man at my age?

Yes. Paradoxically, it may be the saddest day of your life when you do, because your next thought could be, "Oh God, what did I miss all those years!" But seriously, you *deserve* a sexual relationship. Don't be ashamed of your needs.

In terms of adjustment, it's not just sex that's the issue, it's intimacy, and intimacy goes far beyond sex. Authorities note that the most intimate act two people can share is sleeping together in the same bed without sex. The key, of course, is trust and mutual respect. Concentrate on that and the rest will happen naturally.

Do you think a couple should live together before getting married?

A friend of mine who lives in California recently married for the second time. She told me very bluntly, "I wouldn't marry him until we went on a month's trip together. Only when that was over did I know he was the one."

I think that's fine. You have to use care in choosing a mate. Don't be so concerned about public opinion. Don't bother with the fears that if you live with a man your children will stop speaking to you and your friends will whisper behind your back. You deserve to live as you see fit. Do what feels comfortable.

How about choosing to live with a man instead of marrying him?

If you're a senior, that may be a very practical choice. Many seniors live together because they can't afford to marry and thus have one partner forfeit Social Security. I don't believe it's wrong if you love each other and choose to be together rather than alone. Expressions of love are never wrong.

How do I avoid being a fifth wheel when I get together with my married friends?

I tell married women to ask themselves, before they go out for dinner with Marian and Paul or after their card game with Frank and Bev, "If my husband weren't here, would I still be welcome? Would I be having a good time?"

If the answer is no, I tell them that these people are acquaintances, not friends—and that it's important to know the difference between the two. True friends will always desire your company.

And don't forget that one of the secrets to not feeling like a fifth wheel is to reciprocate when people entertain you—just as you did when you were married.

What do you think about older women who go with younger men?

More power to them, the old devils! Seriously, it's always been considered acceptable for older men to go out with younger women. Why discriminate against women in this matter?

How about using escort services?

That's okay, too, as long as you take care that the service is reputable. If you're going to an affair and would like to have a man on your arm, why not?

My favorite response to this question came from "Dear Abby." A woman wrote to her and asked: "What do you think of a wealthy widow who picks up the tab for an escort twenty years her junior who couldn't possibly afford to take her to the places she's accustomed to going? In his line of work he could never treat her on his salary. There can't possibly be any romance in this combination, but he is attractive, flatters her, dances with her, and she seems to enjoy the setup, while he's taking her for all she's worth. Why can't some women realize there is more dignity in sitting home than buying an escort?"

Abby's reply was priceless. She wrote: "I take it you are sitting home. Perhaps this woman also sat home long enough to have concluded that she didn't like it. All that is necessary for a successful relationship is that two people 'need' each other. She needs him. And he needs her. And as long as they aren't hurting anybody, who am I to judge them? And who are you?"

How do you get over the fear of dying alone?

I know what you mean. Maybe you're even a little resentful because your husband had your hand to hold when he died, but you don't have his. But I don't think you have to look at dying alone as a negative thing at all. Let's face it, even if you have your loved ones at your side, this is one trip you're taking by yourself anyway.

You come into the world alone and you die alone. But not entirely. Although I'm not a religious person in the traditional sense, I do feel that our faith in the power of God will allow us to make a peaceful, brave exit from this world into the next, and we can take great comfort in that. I'm rather looking forward to seeing who and what is on the other side!

What can women do to prepare themselves for their loneliness later in life?

They can start by making room in their lives for themselves, for their own needs and desires. Recently I spoke in Hawaii to the wives of businessmen attending a convention. These were women in their forties and fifties who voiced their overwhelming concern to me that their lives lacked creative direction. They admitted that their lives revolved too much around their husbands.

I told them, "It's time to take stock of your emotional assets and to evaluate the net worth of your emotions."

One of the husbands came up to me later and said in a complaining manner, "What did you do to my wife? I've never seen her like this." I replied, "I just reminded her that she is a person in her own right."

Men are sometimes threatened when they see their women blossoming. Growth and change are a necessary part of any good relationship.

I want to get on with my life, but my friends expect me to play the role of the grieving widow. What do I tell them?

The only thing a true friend wants is for you to be happy, so I have to question what kind of friends these are. Women tell me that some of their friends actually act envious—they too would like the opportunity to start a new life! But these aren't friends, they're snakes in the grass.

If you were a good and loving wife and your husband is gone now, you owe nobody an explanation about how you choose to live your life.

What respect do you owe the departed? To continue on and live the kind of life your husband would have wanted you to live.

How can you begin to develop self-esteem?

Accomplishment gives you self-esteem. If you do something for charity or go to a nursing home and cheer someone up who is sad, you'll be surprised by your sense of accomplishment. I know a woman who volunteers in a hospital by pushing the gift cart around from floor to floor. One week she was out for a couple of days and upon her return, one of the patients said, "I was asking where you were! I was concerned that you might be ill. It just wasn't the same without you here."

She had really developed a relationship with that patient, and that can yield the most wonderful feelings of self-worth.

I have a friend who has been very moody since her husband died. How do I help her to snap out of it?

What you are witnessing is the "tantrum syndrome." It's normal for widows to find themselves getting moody or flying off the handle about little things. Many women repressed their moods while married, because they felt their husbands couldn't cope with them.

In many ways these expressions can be healthy, because they signal the beginning of a new awareness. Don't be too hard on your friend. She needs some room to feel what she feels.

Isn't it selfish to put yourself first?

On the contrary. It's about time you did! Your needs have probably always taken a backseat to those of your husband and children. Think of this as your turn now.

Is it possible to keep your sense of humor through the bad times?

How can you *not* laugh at the peculiarities of life? Life is a roller coaster ride of ups and downs. Without humor, it's impossible to enjoy the ride.

Some time ago I developed a way of talking about the uncertain quality of my life. I decided that I had *tsuris*. Those of you who know Yiddish understand exactly what I mean by that. If you've never heard of *tsuris*, let me describe it in this way:

You're walking down the street and a man runs by and grabs your purse. You start to chase him and fall into an open manhole. While you're lying there, a snake crawls over and bites you. Finally, when the firemen come to pull you out, they drop you and you break your leg in seven places. People will say, "She has *tsuris!*" Can you see the humor in this? I've always viewed my life as a comedy of errors, with an emphasis on the *comedy*. I'm telling you, it helps.

My husband was an alcoholic and in the last years of his life, I resented him so much I was almost glad to see him go. Now I feel guilty.

Alcoholism is a terrible disease, and those who haven't been through it can't understand the pain of families that have an alcoholic member. I assume that you weren't involved in one of the wonderful family support programs like Al-Anon, which would have helped you deal with your feelings and realize that the situation was not your fault. You cannot be blamed for your feelings of relief now that this burden is gone. Guilt will only cripple you now. Put the past behind you and concentrate on your future.

Incidentally, it is only very recently that there has been any real support available for the families of alcoholics. Nowadays it is understood that alcoholism is a family disease that makes everyone suffer.

But ask yourself: Haven't you suffered enough?

How could you live with yourself after putting your husband in a nursing home?

Sending Harry to the Actors' Home was the hardest thing I've ever had to do. I had all the normal feelings: fear that I was just trying to unload a burden... questions about how I could do this to someone I really loved... guilt about abandoning him. This was a man I had been married to for forty years, my most intimate companion and partner. And I was sending him away.

At the time, I felt I had no choice. He was too sick for me to care for him, and I had to work to support us. But that didn't make it any easier.

What I learned, though, as I've said earlier, was that nursing homes are not necessarily bad. Harry loved the Actors' Home. He was less isolated there than he would have been in our apartment. He made many friends and was well treated there. Don't automatically assume that nursing homes are depressing places where people just sit around and wait to die. Investigate the options. You can find out about homes and hospice programs by calling the outreach center of your local hospital.

One final note. Sometimes the things we do in the name of love don't, on the surface, appear loving and self-less. But when you examine your heart, you'll know what's right.

Recommended Reading

There are a number of worthwhile books and publications that can help you get through your grief and move on to enjoy a satisfying, healthy, rewarding life. The following are some of my favorites.

Books

HANDLING GRIEF
How to Survive the Loss of a Love
By Harold H. Bloomfield, M.D.; Melba Colgrove, Ph.D.; and Peter McWilliams
Bantam Books (paperback edition), 1980.
A moving and inspirational guide to help you regain your sense of self after suffering a loss.

Formerly Married: Learning to Live with Yourself
By Marilyn Jensen
Bridgebooks, Westminster, 1983.
The author incorporates her own story into this
courageous and practical guide to learning to live alone.

Second Chance
By Syd Banks
Fawcett Books, 1987.
A moving little book that traces the journey of one man to
discover the miraculous power of mind over matter.

Living with an Empty Chair: A Guide Through Grief
By Dr. Roberta Temes
Irvington Publishers, Inc., 1984.
A step-by-step guide to getting through your grief—
sensitive and straightforward.

The Courage to Grieve
By Judy Tatelbaum
Harper & Row, 1980.
A guide to facing up to your grief and moving on to a new
phase of life.

LIVING FULLY AS A SENIOR

Single After Fifty
By Adeline McConnell and Beverly Anderson
McGraw Hill (paper), 1980.
A practical, helpful book for people facing the single
jitters at a later age.

Success over Sixty
By Albert Myers and Christopher P. Andersen
Simon & Schuster, Summit, 1984.
Nuts and bolts suggestions for opening new career vistas
in later years.

Enjoy Old Age: Living Fully in Your Senior Years
By B. F. Skinner & M. E. Vaughan
Norton, 1983.
The noted behaviorist offers a solid and uplifting view of the benefits of living your "golden years."

Life Begins at Sixty
By Bill Case
Stein & Day, 1985.
Packed with examples and "proof positive" that the later years can be the best years. Includes hundreds of ideas for starting over.

Our Best Years
By Helen Hayes, with Marion Glasserow Gladney
Doubleday, 1986.
Beautifully written and inspiring words from one of America's leading ladies.

BEING FIT AND HEALTHY
Enjoy Sex in the Middle Years
By Christine E. Sandford, M.D.
Arco Publishing, 1983.
A sensitively written guide to happy, healthy sex in the later years.

Fitness After Fifty
By Herbert DeVries, Ph.D., with Dianne Hales
Scribner, 1987.
A detailed exercise manual for lifelong health and fitness.

The Nutritional Ages of Women
By Patricia Long
Bantam Books (paperback edition), 1986.
A study of how your nutritional needs change as you grow

older—guidelines for building your healthiest menu
plans.

Stop Stress and Aging Now
By Dr. David C. Gardner and Dr. Grace Joely Beatty
American Training and Research Associates, Publishers,
1985.
A workbook-style manual to insure your top-notch
condition.

Periodicals
Modern Maturity
Published bimonthly by the American Association of
Retired Persons, 1909 K Street, N.W., Washington, DC
20049.

Gray Panther Network
Published bimonthly by the Gray Panthers, 3635
Chestnut Street, Philadelphia, PA 19104.

Senior Guardian
Published bimonthly by the National Association of
Senior Citizens, 2525 Wilson Boulevard, Arlington, VA
22201.

Our Age
Published bimonthly by the National Association of
Senior Citizens, 2525 Wilson Boulevard, Arlington, VA
22201.

Senior Citizen News
Published monthly by the National Council of Senior
Citizens, 925 15th Street N.W., Washington, DC 20005.

About the Author

Virginia Graham, television, radio, and theater celebrity, was hostess of the ABC television series *Girl Talk* and the nationally syndicated *Virginia Graham Show* for more than fifteen seasons. She continues to appear on daytime dramas, including *All My Children*. The author of four previous books, Virginia Graham lectures widely around the country and is nationally recognized as a leading charity fundraiser and spokesperson on many issues concerning American women. She lives in New York City.